T0289383

Human izing Strategy

Geert Vercaeren

How to Master Emotions, Values and Beliefs When You Execute Plans

Lannoo
Campus

To all who inspired me,
and all I wish to inspire

Contents

CHAPTER 3

Humanizing CULTURE shifts   116

CHAPTER 4

Humanizing LEADERSHIP   172

Introduction

'When you change the way you look at things,
 the things you look at change.'
— Max Planck

Why this book?

During my 25-year career as business consultant, coach, and executive in leading consulting firms, I have become painfully aware of the challenges of realizing strategies successfully. I have witnessed first-hand the ineffectiveness of many organizations and their inability to execute even the most well thought out strategies.

> *With so much literature published on the subject, all the best practices available, and so many consulting firms out there, why do most strategies still fail?*

It's not a secret that most organizations struggle with strategy execution. Strategy execution is complex. Roughly 70 percent of efforts at transformation fail. People in organizations struggle to focus on the right priorities, fail to act in accordance with the strategic objectives, or simply do not engage with the vision of the CEO. Often, people are not convinced about the importance and urgency of the changes and simply do not buy-in to it. Leadership not setting sufficiently high aspirations and the lack of investment in critical skills, capabilities and behaviors (culture) are other major reasons why efforts at transformation fall short of desired results.

The current development towards digitalization and ecosystems that comprise many different parties will only increase complexity. The financial losses resulting from failed strategy implementation are tremendous, not to mention the operational and emotional disruption to the organization and its people.

What if you could lead an organization where plans and decisions are executed; where a team acts as 'one team'; where people work together spontaneously across teams? What if you could lead an organization where people are inspired and committed to the strategy? What if you could build an organization with efficiency, values, trust and fun at its heart?

> *'Thinking is easy, acting is difficult, and to put one's thoughts into*
> *action is the most difficult thing in the world.'*
> – Johann Wolfgang von Goethe

Values, beliefs and emotions have a proven impact on human motivation and thus influence our focus, decisions and actions. Yet these elements are often neglected in the professional world, thereby dehumanizing strategies and organizations.

Leading research shows that emotion-based barriers present a major threat to strategy execution within organizations. Mistrust and low sharing of useful and timely information, low receptivity to effortful change, mechanistic actions and complacency are examples of barriers that prevent the sense of urgency and commitment which is necessary for change to prevail.

Emotional and psychological factors are often neglected in the strategic process, but they have a significant impact on the performance of your organization and the successful realization of strategies. I believe there are several reasons for this. Lack of knowledge and risk aversion of senior management play a role, but so does anxiety about dealing with emotions. In short, our dominant professional logic often does not include emotions.

> *No business strategy can afford to neglect emotional and psychological*
> *factors, because all strategies ultimately deal with people.*

In my experience, executing a strategy effectively requires going beyond fixing symptoms or introducing expensive short-term technical solutions. Interventions should start by exploring the root causes of the observed behaviours and integrating a solid business perspective complemented by psychology-informed approaches based on scientific tools. I strongly believe in an approach that focuses on visible technical elements such as structure, governance, process and tools. Simultaneously, it is critical to tap into the world of values, beliefs, emotions and hidden underlying motivational forces that influence individual and collective behaviour.

My personal mission and the mission of the company I founded (B15) is to work with leaders to solve their most critical issues by including human-centred strategies that work in their unique context. I want to have a different conversation with leaders and offer them a different approach to strategy execution.

This book provides you with new insights, an unconventional approach on how to humanize your organization and make your strategy really work. Based on leading research, real stories, case studies and practical tools, I will take you into the world of values, beliefs, emotions and often hidden underlying motivational forces that influence individual and collective behaviours in organizations. I will show how dealing consciously and effectively with these human dynamics can have a significant impact on the performance of your organization and the successful realization of your strategy.

Take a quick test to check if this book is for you; answer the following questions with Yes or No:

1. Are you serious about making your strategy a success?
2. Do you have the patience to keep asking 'why'?
3. Do you have the courage to take a less conventional approach?

If you answered YES to these questions, you will find this book inspiring and useful.

The structure of this book

Why is so much time, effort and energy in teams sidetracked by emotions, tensions and conflicts? Why don't we get rid of the silos within my organization? Why don't people in my organization act and focus in accordance with our strategic objectives? Why don't people in my organization engage with the vision I shared? Why is my organization not ready to deal effectively with the rapidly changing challenges?

These are examples of recurring challenges and frustrations that leaders of organizations share with me on a daily basis.

I am convinced by my experience that it is possible to deal with these challenges that often block the realization of their ambitions, aspirations and related strategies. It is possible to build high-performing teams, to make people work together spontaneously across teams, to make people act and focus in line with the strategy, to inspire and create commitment to strategy and to build a (more) future-proof organization.

What are your **challenges?**	What do you **hope** for?
Why is so much time, effort and energy of team members sidetracked by emotions, tensions and conflicts?	**What if** the team acts as ONE team?
Why don't we get rid of the silos within my organization?	**What if** the people in my organization work together spontaneously across teams?
Why do people in my organization not act and focus in accordance with our strategic objectives?	**What if** people act and focus in line with the strategy, set the right priorities and execute plans and decisions taken?
Why do people in my organization not engage with the vision I shared?	**What if** I could inspire and create commitment to the strategy from within the organization?
Why is my organization not ready to deal effectively with the rapidly changing challenges?	**What if** I could build a future-proof organization based on efficiency, values, trust and fun?

Five key challenges and hopes of leaders

This book is structured around these five challenges (frustrations, fears) and hopes (ambitions, aspirations) of today's leaders.

It will give you insights and practical tools on how to deal with these critical challenges by taking a human-centred approach; it will show you how to humanize your strategy and make it really work.

The picture below visualizes the basic logic and structure of the book and explains how applying human-centred tactics in these five different domains will significantly increase the success rate of your strategy execution.

5 challenges	HUMANIZING	5 hopes	IN THE BOOK	
Much time, effort and energy of team members is sidetracked by emotions, tensions and conflicts	→ 3 human-centred tactics →	A teams acts as ONE team	→ CHAPTER 1 Humanizing TEAM performance →	
Geting rid of the silos within my organization	→ 3 human-centred tactics →	The people in my organization work together spontaneously across teams	→ CHAPTER 2 Humanizing COLLABORATION across teams →	Increased success rate of your strategy execution →
People in my organization do not act and focus in accordance with our strategic objectives	→ 3 human-centred tactics →	People act and focus in line with the strategy, set the right priorities and execute plans and decisions taken	→ CHAPTER 3 Humanizing CULTURE shifts →	
People in my organization do not engage with the vision I shared	→ 3 human-centred tactics →	I inspire and create commitment to the strategy from within the organization	→ CHAPTER 4 Humanizing LEADERSHIP →	
My organization is not ready to deal effectively with the rapidly changing challenges	→ 3 human-centred tactics →	I have a future-proof organization based on efficiency, values, trust and fun	→ CHAPTER 5 Humanizing future-proof ORGANIZATIONS →	

The logic of this book

Each of the chapters is structured in a similar way: in five parts. They start with 'why it matters': how the topic impacts the success of your organization (part 1). As there is already a lot of literature on this question, I do not elaborate extensively on this and provide you with a short personal perspective based on my experience. Afterwards I tell you a story about a project, initiative or intervention I conducted (part 2) followed by three less conventional, human-centred tactics that I experienced as highly impactful in dealing with this challenge (part 3). Each chapter ends with a summary of the main points (part 4) and gives you some practical instructions on how to get started (part 5). I also provide a list of key references and interesting additional reads on this topic.

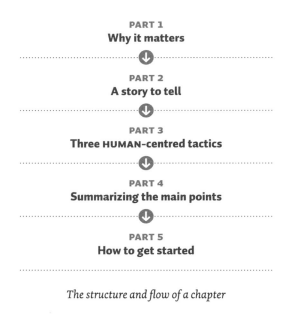

The structure and flow of a chapter

In each chapter, you will also discover an illustration created by the artist Peter Moolan-Feroze, which shows his artistic interpretation of the topic. He has also constructed a short narrative around some of the key messages in the five chapters of this book. They explain the ideas behind the drawings, which all explore different human aspects of performance in organizations.

CHAPTER 1

Humanizing TEAM performance

Effective teamwork is identified as one of the core practices in high-performing organizations. The ability to quickly build, deploy, disband, and reform teams is a critical skill for today's organizations. The story *'From Me to We'* shows that effort and time within teams is easily sidetracked by emotions, tensions, and conflicts. Unconscious dynamics are often a source of ineffectiveness in a team. I elaborate on three less conventional, human-centred tactics, which I found highly impactful in building high-performing teams. Finally, I will provide you with practical tools to get started on acting as ONE team.

CHAPTER 2

Humanizing COLLABORATION across teams

Inter-group collaboration is often ineffective. It does not create the intended value and even destroys company value. In this chapter, we discuss the highly complex phenomenon of collaboration. The story *'Us versus Them'* shows that although the start of a collaboration can be conscious and rational, the process is often influenced by hidden emotional and unconscious motives and dynamics. I elaborate on three less conventional, human-centred tactics that, in my experience, are highly impactful in helping teams to work together. Finally, I will provide you with practical tools to start getting rid of your silos.

CHAPTER 3

Humanizing CULTURE shifts

'The way we do things around here', or the culture of an organization, exerts a powerful influence on its success. Defining your desired culture is not that difficult. The story *'Who needs to change first?'* shows that the proof of the pudding is in the eating; embedding new behaviours is a challenging journey, but achievable. I elaborate on three less conventional, human-centred tactics that I have seen to be highly impactful to shift towards desired behaviours supporting your strategy. Finally, I will provide you with practical tools to start getting your people to behave in line with your strategic objectives.

CHAPTER 4
Humanizing LEADERSHIP

If the leadership dimension is not properly in place, organizations simply cannot be successful. Effective leadership corresponds directly with organizational performance; a single change in the behaviour of a leader can trigger a significant impact on the performance of the business, either positively or negatively. The story *'Uncomfortable reflections'* shows that reflection is not part of the dominant logic in our (professional) lives and that self-awareness is the essential starting point to trigger potential shifts in mindset and behaviour as a leader. I elaborate on three less conventional, human-centred tactics that I experienced as highly impactful for leaders in inspiring and creating commitment to the strategy from within the organization. Finally, I will provide practical tools to get you started in making this happen.

CHAPTER 5
Humanizing future-proof ORGANIZATIONS

Organizations today operate in the context of increased complexity, uncertainty, and continuous change. How future work is organized within organizations and within the broader ecosystems is a significant accelerator in the performance of organizations. It significantly impacts future value creation, staying relevant and survival. The story *'Speed, Gears and Brakes'* shows how to build an organization that is able to deal effectively with the challenges of rapid change and to stay relevant in the future. I elaborate on three less conventional, human-centred tactics that are highly impactful in building future-proof organizations. Then, I will give you the toolkit for building your future-proof organization based on efficiency, values, trust, and fun.

CHAPTER 6

Bringing it all together

This chapter brings the five previous chapters together; it is a summary of how to humanize the realization of your strategy from a methodological perspective. I describe the five critical steps of the methodology and approach to humanize strategies. I elaborate on the socio-technical approach, which combines a structural, technical perspective with a psychological perspective focusing on human dynamics (systems psychodynamics). I also emphasize on the critical role of the leader, and of the consultant/coach as external facilitator, in this process.

My concluding letter to you as a leader

I end the book with a letter to you as a leader, in which I share some final thoughts and give you my final piece of advice.

How to read this book

This book is built up in a way that allows you to read it as a whole or as separate parts. Each chapter is a module on its own.

To explore the relevance of the different parts in your specific context, you might want to use one of the two questionnaires below in order to set your reading priorities. You can choose the angle you like to set priorities: challenges (questionnaire 1) in case you would like to start from your pain points, or hopes (questionnaire 2) in case you would like to start from your ambitions and aspirations.

QUESTIONNAIRE 1
Your challenges in order of priority

Looking at my organization today, the biggest challenges we have in realizing our strategy are:

- ☐ Much time, effort and energy of team members is sidetracked by emotions, tensions and conflicts *(chapter 1)*.
- ☐ Getting rid of the silos within my organization *(chapter 2)*.
- ☐ People in my organization do not act and focus in accordance with our strategic objectives *(chapter 3)*.
- ☐ People in my organization do not engage with the vision I shared *(chapter 4)*.
- ☐ My organization is not ready to deal effectively with the rapidly changing challenges *(chapter 5)*.

Rank the statements you selected, based on the impact that dealing with these challenges will have on successfully realizing your strategy. You might want to start reading the chapters in this order.

Your priorities of hope

Looking at my organization today, investing in one or more of the following areas will have a positive impact on the successful realization of our strategy:

- ☐ A team acts as ONE team *(chapter 1)*.
- ☐ The people in my organization work together spontaneously across teams *(chapter 2)*.
- ☐ People act and focus in line with the strategy, set the right priorities and execute plans and decisions taken *(chapter 3)*.
- ☐ I inspire and create commitment to the strategy from within the organization *(chapter 4)*.
- ☐ I have a future-proof organization based on efficiency, values, trust and fun *(chapter 5)*.

Rank the statements you selected, based on the impact they will have on successfully realizing your strategy. You might want to start reading the chapters in this order.

CHAPTER 1

Humanizing TEAM performance

A HUMAN-centred approach to building
high-performing teams

'It is amazing what can be
accomplished when nobody cares
about who gets the credit.'
– Robert Yates

Why is so much time, effort and energy of team members sidetracked by emotions, tensions and conflicts?

YOUR HOPE

**What if the team acts
as ONE team?**

Why it matters

Effective teamwork is identified by many researchers as one of the core practices in high-performing organizations. Teams are an important way to distribute and organize work in organizations. The essence of effective teamwork is to create a product or deliver a service through a collective effort that exceeds the quality of an individual endeavour. Teams typically capitalize on the benefits of offering diversity, promoting learning opportunities, facilitating complex problem solving, flexibility, faster delivery of results and so on.

The ability to quickly build, deploy, disband, and reform teams is a critical skill for today's organizations.

For example, savvy investors in start-ups often value the quality of the team and the interaction of the founding members more than the idea. According to a McKinsey study, 90 percent of investors think the quality of the management team is the single most important non-financial factor when evaluating an IPO. There also seems to be a 1.9 times greater likelihood of having above-median financial performance when the top team is working together towards a common vision.

The shift from hierarchies to cross-functional teams is well underway. Organizations are decentralizing authority, moving towards product- and customer-centric organizations, and forming dynamic networks of highly empowered teams that communicate and coordinate activities in unique and powerful ways.

A story to tell: From 'me' to 'we'

After my Executive Master studies in Organizational Psychology at INSEAD in 2015, I had an interview with a journalist from a business magazine. He was interested in my most recent research on how drawings can help in interventions to improve inter-group collaboration. After the publication of the article, the CEO of a Small to Medium Enterprise, Bart, called me for help in dealing with a business challenge he had been facing for many years.

Bart described his challenges and hopes in a comprehensive briefing document.

Bart and I met a week later, and we had an in-depth discussion about the challenges he was facing. He had created a comprehensive briefing document including the company's mission, business model, financial figures, market opportunities, his perception of the different leadership team member profiles and their ambitions. In short, he saw plenty of opportunities to grow his business, but was really struggling with the leadership team and the conflicted relationships between the team members. Bart explained that his leadership team consisted of five people (including himself) who had been engaged in ongoing conflict for almost four years.

The leadership team was so dysfunctional that this prevented them from grasping opportunities.

He and the other members of the leadership team were distant, and there was a lot of frustration between them. They did not talk to one another outside of meetings organized by Bart. All contact was highly emotional and discussions ended up in non-constructive dialogue and led to personal struggles and competition in which the focus and energy was directed at 'who wins' instead of the content, task or solution that was involved. Overall, the level of trust was extremely low between all the team members. Because of the long-standing conflicts, all discussions took place in one-on-one meetings with the CEO. Bart reached out to me for support because he believed that an external expert and a more psychological approach could (hopefully) solve the painful issues he was facing.

The safe setting helped to liberate the huge stress and hopelessness he had felt for many years.

Bart was very open and emotional about the situation. I could sense his desperation about the situation in every word. He had already taken many different steps (for example, team meetings, which had ended in explicit conflicts) to solve the issue but he had not succeeded. He felt very lonely in dealing with this issue, and felt that he had failed. Bart also made it clear that his physical health was suffering as a result of the situation. I listened to this very painful situation for hours. I could feel the sustained pressure he had been under for a long time. He had taken over the company from his father 10 years ago and was the only shareholder of the company. Bart was very emotionally connected to his company; it was 'his baby' and a crucial part of his identity. He intended to sell the company within the following two to three years, but he wanted to fix the problem with the leadership team first.

We started an initiative to build a future-poof leadership team.

Based on this emotional initial meeting, I developed an approach with a focus on the growth ambitions of the company combined with the creation of self-awareness in the team members and their interpersonal dynamics. We stated the ambition to build a leadership team that acted with trust and respect for one another, that shared the same ambitions, discussed the future openly, and that was more self-directed. Bart and I agreed upfront that my approach was likely to trigger tipping points and reactions from the team members that would be hard to predict. We both had the confidence that this was what was needed to be done to get out of this painful situation.

During the kick-off meeting, I experienced the extreme brokenness of the team and the pain it had caused.

The first step was to bring the leadership team together to kick off and position the initiative, make some practical arrangements, and to do an initial observation on the functioning of the broken team. This was the first time I met the team. Compared to other team coaching, I found the level of dysfunction rather extreme. I observed a very high level of tension between some of the team members and could imagine how a lot of effort, energy and time was dedicated to dealing with emotions instead of dealing with the business activities at hand. I also observed a lot of restrained emotions and passive-aggressive behaviour at different times during the meeting. The key objective of this kick-off meeting was to clearly state that the current situation was unacceptable, that something needed to happen and that I would work together with them to support this journey.

> *Taking the time to create awareness about their own functioning and that of the team was a crucial first step.*

Because of this first observation, I decided to start by talking to each of the leadership team members separately. I conducted two one-on-one sessions with each of them. The objective of the first session was to increase self-awareness and insights on personal strengths, behavioural roadblocks, motivation, interpersonal relationships, and potential recurring conflict patterns. During the second session, I focused on the functioning of the team from different perspectives. To facilitate these two meetings, I used quantitative methods with a focus on their personality profile, personal values, and a team effectiveness assessment in which I applied Lencioni's model, which is based on five dysfunctions of a team. It outlines the root causes of politics and dysfunction in teams (absence of trust, fear of conflict, lack of commitment, avoidance of accountability and inattention to results), and the keys to overcoming them. No surprise that the scores of the latter assessment indicated that results, accountability, commitment, conflict, and trust were low and areas of concern for this team (see figure opposite).

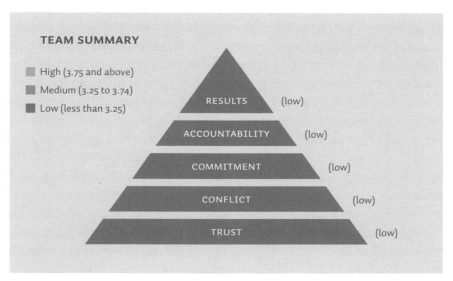

TEAM SUMMARY

High (3.75 and above)
Medium (3.25 to 3.74)
Low (less than 3.25)

RESULTS (low)

ACCOUNTABILITY (low)

COMMITMENT (low)

CONFLICT (low)

TRUST (low)

Lencioni team effectiveness results (high level) (Source: The Table Group / Lencioni)

Examples of more qualitative tools I applied were drawing a self-portrait and drawing the current and then the ideal, desired leadership team. I am a big advocate of using drawings as they provide an enormous amount of rich data on conscious and unconscious experiences within the team in a remarkably effective manner.

Examples of a drawing of the self-portrait of a leader (1) and the perceived leadership team today (2)

The drawing of the self-portrait on page 31 is an example of the self-portrait of one of the leaders. The drawing represents her in three different moments (in the past, on the left; today, in the middle; and in future, on the right). We discovered that independence and being able to speak up (from the gut) are important to her. The person on the right side of this picture also represents her boss and mentor who she appreciates, looks up to and is a real role model overall. She feels she is growing and her ambition is to become like her boss.

As a next step, I prepared a team coaching intervention. The objectives were to increase trust, to resolve conflict constructively, to foster greater commitment and accountability within the team, to define action areas and to plan to improve team effectiveness (including quick wins). The coaching intervention took place in a quiet place. At the start of the session, the company's vision, direction, and ambitions were made very clear. Bart also made it clear that the commitment to this direction as well as the personal commitment to be willing to improve collaboration within the team were non-negotiables if team members were to remain part of the future leadership team.

From 'me' to 'we' was the mental shift the team needed to make.

A key element of the preparation of the workshop was a note I had created, with observations and hypotheses on the interpersonal dynamics and their explanation based on the kick-off meeting observation and individual sessions. I presented this working note to the team members during the workshop and positioned it as input for discussion.

Examples of observations I shared with them were:

- Perseverance is usually strongly present within your own area of responsibility. To a limited extent, you have a strategic and overarching perspective, but little initiative is taken, and this is certainly outside your own area of responsibility.
- Insights into the activities of others is usually done indirectly and mainly through the CEO.
- The CEO follows up briefly with individual team members on a daily basis.
- Discussing personal matters, shortcomings, areas of development and failures is out of the question.

- When contact takes place between team members, this is usually accompanied by many emotions and frustrations. In case of confrontation, opinions are expressed but usually end in non-constructive dialogue (which is a repetitive pattern). Dialogues often lead to a personal struggle or competition in which the focus and energy goes to 'who wins' instead of to the content, task or solution that is involved.
- It is not clear how decisions are made and who is involved in these decisions.
- Team members give each other limited direct, explicit feedback (positive or points for improvement).
- Criticism is difficult to accept and the responsibility for finding a solution is usually placed on the other person instead of him/herself.
- Very strong focus on yourselves with little interest in the overarching, strategic business goal. Focus is on 'ME', not 'WE'.

The potential explanations and hypotheses about these dynamics I shared with them were as follows:

- The survival dilemma plays out in the tension to protect yourself (self-preservation, protection of own identity) versus the need to collaborate and interact with others. The persistent tensions within the organization, the frustrations with regard to the functioning of the team, as well as the uncertainty with regard to your future role within the company are elements activating even more extreme focus on the protection of your own identity (isolation, falling back on yourself).
- There is a great deal of distrust towards one another especially in the perception of intention and integrity (not so much in terms of competence). The difference in personal values may be the basis for this. Being vulnerable is perceived as giving 'ammunition' to the other and can lead to personal losses (which might be perceived as a threat to identity).
- The strategy, future evolution/potential sale of the company, common objective(s), expectations of one another, common ground on which to cooperate and decision-making processes have not been made explicit.
- There is a perception of dishonesty – that certain people are protected and promoted.

- There are many assumptions and misunderstandings about one another that are not checked against reality (partly due to limited personal contact) and cause repetitive dysfunctional behaviour.
- The threat to your identity and the need for personal recognition activates (unconscious) protective mechanisms in self defence. Examples of reactions are: minimizing contact, urge to compare and distinguish yourself, perseverance in your own area of responsibility, not being vulnerable, competition/confrontation, fleeing, intellectualization, control.

Tipping points were triggered and led to impactful decisions and changes in behaviour.

From the start of the initiative, and especially during the workshop, Bart and I increased the pressure regarding two personal commitments from each team member: the personal commitment towards the growth strategy of the organization on one hand, and the commitment to be willing to improve the functioning of the team on the other hand. During the second day of the team coaching intervention, things started to change. One leader decided to leave the company as he became aware that he could not find himself in the future direction and values of the organization. Other team members were committed to the future strategy and shared their commitment to further developing themselves and the interaction between team members.

After the session, I kept supporting the individual team members and the team to fully embed and reinforce the new behaviours. We kept investing heavily in building trust and psychological safety within the team. One and a half years later, I met Bart again and he came across as very relaxed. It became clear that the interventions conducted created the necessary breakthroughs. The growth agenda had been realized and he was having multiple conversations about the sale of his business. A critical business issue was solved by including human-centred tactics. I was enormously proud to have been part of putting this organization back on track to realize its growth ambitions.

Three HUMAN-centred tactics

In the section below, I share three human-centred tactics that I found highly impactful in creating high-performing teams:

1. Invest in understanding the human dynamics within the team and its impact on performance.
2. Never stop investing in trust and psychological safety.
3. Conduct team coaching interventions in a safe and reflective setting.

Below I elaborate on each of the three human-centred tactics in more detail.

TACTIC 1

Invest in understanding the human dynamics within the team and its impact on performance

---

THE HIDDEN HUMAN DYNAMICS WITHIN TEAMS

A lot has been written about human, interpersonal dynamics within teams. Below, I will share some dynamics that I often encounter in teams. Based on some concrete examples, I will also elaborate on their potential root cause and the impact they might have on team performance.

> *The survival dilemma of team members is often a source of ineffectiveness of teams.*

As explained in Bart's story, the survival dilemma played an important role in the functioning of this leadership team. The survival of any system – whether individual or group – depends on the interactions with its environment. This creates the dilemma: How can I maintain a sense of identity and continuity as a person (leading to preservation and isolation), and at the same time contribute to, and receive from others (leading to connection and integration)? These persistent tensions within the team, the frustrations with regard to the functioning of the team, as well as the uncertainty about their future role within the company were contextual elements activating even more extreme focus on the protection of their own identity (isolation, falling back on oneself). As a result, team members put an extreme focus on the 'me' rather than on the 'we'.

> *How much time and effort of team members is sidetracked by emotions, tensions and conflicts?*

As a consequence of this, all kinds of protective mechanisms were activated to deal with this self-preservation or maintenance of self-esteem, like minimizing contact (avoidance), the urge to compare and distinguish, perseverance in their own domain of responsibility, not showing vulnerability, competition/confrontation, flight, intellectualization and extreme control.

Needless to say, these reactions did not help them to be effective as a team. They often led to a loss of efficiency (time and energy, reduced productivity) as well as a reduction in morale and motivation. As a result, the team was incited to 'off-tasks', which means that team members put effort, energy and time into dealing with these negative emotions and frustrations instead of focusing on the primary (business) task of the team.

While Bart's leadership team operated individualistically, there is another dynamic that can also have negative effects. Groupthink is a dynamic that I often encounter within teams.

> *Groupthink causes a group to minimize conflict and reach consensus without critical evaluation of the decision.*

This psychological phenomenon occurs within a group in which the desire for harmony or conformity results in an irrational or dysfunctional decision-making outcome. Cohesiveness, or the desire for cohesiveness, in a group may produce a tendency among its members to agree at all costs. This causes the group to minimize conflict and reach consensus without critical evaluation of the decision. How do you detect groupthink? What are potential symptoms of groupthink pathology? Some examples:

- Illusion of invulnerability; excessive optimism and encouragement to take big risks;
- Efforts to rationalize or to discount warnings, or negative information that might lead them to reconsider the group's assumptions;
- Unquestioning belief in the group's inherent morality; inclining members to ignore ethical and moral consequences of their decisions;
- Stereotyped views of competitors and enemies as too evil, too immoral, too weak or stupid to effectively obstruct the group's purposes;
- Direct pressure on persons holding deviant opinions, views or data; 'dissidence destroys loyalty';
- Self-censorship of deviations from the apparent group consensus or minimizing the importance of doubts and counter arguments;
- Emergence of self-appointed 'mind-guards' to protect the group from adverse information.

Creating awareness about these dynamics is the first step.

The good news is that there are mechanisms to cope with these dynamics. The first step is to become aware of the interpersonal dynamics that support or counteract effective teamwork and to understand their impact. Conducting reality checks on assumptions made about one another as well as increasing trust between team members and developing more empathy (putting themselves in the other team members' shoes) are tactics to improve interpersonal relations. Other ways to improve rapport between team members are focusing on a strong common mission (rational level), reinforcing playfulness/fun, and expressing emotions towards one another (humanizing the team).

EVALUATE THE DNA OF A TEAM ABOVE AND BELOW THE SURFACE

After the kick-off meeting, I usually start by conducting an online survey and in-depth interviews with the different team members. The objective of this step is to discover areas of strength and further development by taking a combined structural and psychological perspective. This leads to a report that will be the starting point for discussion (and for formulating a plan of action) with the team.

The following four areas are typically addressed in the team evaluation:

1. Team engagement, pride, energy, and stress level.
2. Overall team effectiveness of the team.
3. Team values, behaviours, and interpersonal dynamics.
4. Final recommendations (based on the evaluation).

The examples explained below are based on a real team coaching intervention. As you will see, this team was less dysfunctional than the leadership team described in the story earlier and is hopefully more representative of your teams.

Area 1: Team engagement, pride, energy and stress level

Based on the online survey and in-depth interviews, the following qualitative and quantitative data and insights are discovered about the team: 'Team-in-the-mind' being the thoughts and feelings associated with the team, the level of engagement, the drivers of pride, the drivers and drainers of energy, and the level of stress experienced.

Below you will find examples of questions the team members were asked on these different dimensions.

Question asked: Which picture best represents the team today?

Example of pictures representing the team-in-the-mind today (Source: METALOG emotion cards)

In this case, team members associated the project with challenge, persever-ance, commitment, clear goals and direction, freedom, 'one team' and the potential for improvement in its functioning.

Question asked: How do you feel when you think of the team?

Example of the emotional barometer of the team

In this example, the feelings related to the project are diverse: 50% of the team members feel happy or excited while 50% feel worried or frustrated.

Question asked: What are the key drivers of stress for you on the project?

Key drivers of stress	Percentage	
Excessively high workloads, with unrealistic deadlines making me feel rushed, under pressure and overwhelmed	64%	❶
Multiple reporting lines	36%	❷
Lack of control over my work activities	29%	
Micro-management which makes me feel undervalued	29%	❸
Lack of interpersonal support or poor working relationships	14%	
My role on the project does not fit my capabilities, knowledge, personality	7%	
Culture of blame	7%	
Weak or ineffective leadership which leads to a lack of sense of direction	7%	
A negative, toxic working environment (too much attention to power, money and status, little ethical behaviour)	0%	

Example of top three drivers of stress in the team

In this case, the top three key drivers of stress are related to an excessive workload with unrealistic timelines, multiple reporting lines, lack of control over their own work and micro-management.

Question asked: What is the level of stress you experience?

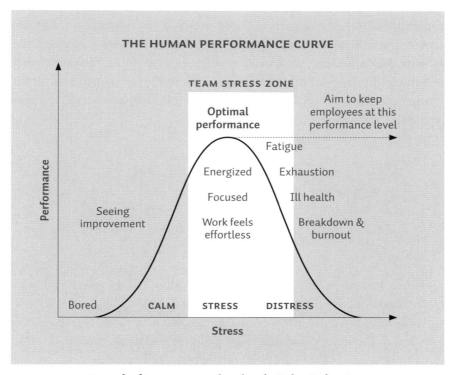

Example of team stress zone based on the Yerkes-Dodson Law

In this example, the level of stress experienced varied significantly between team members: Some members experienced too high levels of stress while others experienced acceptable or low levels of stress. In this case, the level of stress for the team was going to increase. For this reason it was important to (1) create time/space where stress would be openly discussed, (2) understand the individual and team drivers of stress and how this impacts team dynamics and (3) apply structural and behavioural tactics to bring the stress to the optimal performance level.

Area 2: The overall effectiveness of the team

The focus of the below evaluation is to better understand the effectiveness of the team. It is based on Lencioni's model of the five dysfunctions of a team and outlines the root causes of politics and dysfunction on teams (absence of trust, fear of conflict, lack of commitment, avoidance of accountability and inattention to results) and the keys to overcoming them. See below the findings of a team assessment in terms of overall effectiveness and the level of trust.

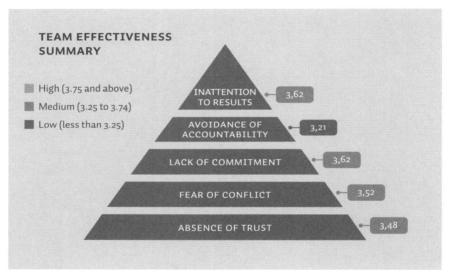

Example of the effectiveness of the team at five levels (Source: The Table Group / Lencioni)

The summary of scores below indicates that results, commitment, conflict, trust and especially accountability are areas of attention to improve the effectiveness of the team. The overall effectiveness score of the team is medium with attention points mainly at the level of 'accountability'. Commitment and result-orientation score highest. Examples of elements that have a positive impact on the effectiveness of the team are related to alignment around common goals, discussion of the most important and difficult issues at meetings, acknowledgement by the team of the contributions and achievements of others. Examples of areas of attention are insufficient censure of unproductive behaviours, lack of timely confrontation of poor performers, and insufficient pressure on them to improve.

The level of trust within the team is strongly defined by the perceived competence of team members (capabilities and results). Insufficient transparency and openness are key characteristics that reduce trust within the team.

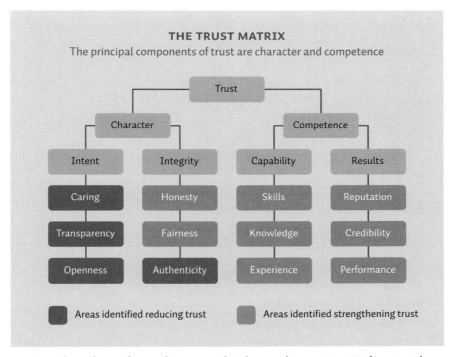

Areas that reduce and strengthen trust within the team (Source: Barrett Values Centre)

Investing in better understanding each other's working style (nr.1), being more forthright, and getting to know each other better on a personal level will create more trust within the team (see the table on the next page).

There would be more trust on the team if we:	Percentage	
understand each other's working style	57%	1
are more forthright with information	50%	2
get to know each other on a personal level	36%	3
spend more time together	29%	
give credit where credit is due	29%	
share professional failures and successes	21%	
let go of grudges	14%	
admit their mistakes	14%	
reduce the amount of gossiping	7%	
readily apologize	7%	

Top three investments to increase trust in the team (Source: Barrett Values Centre)

Area 3: Team values, behaviours and interpersonal dynamics

The focus of this deep dive is on team values, behaviours and interpersonal dynamics.

The power of working with values

Understanding the personal, perceived and desired values of the team gives important insights about the 'glue' connecting team members at a deeper level, how team functioning is experienced currently, potential sources of frustration (so called 'hot buttons') and how the team can reach its highest effectiveness.

Personal values reflect what is important to us. They are a shorthand way of describing our individual motivations. Together with our beliefs, they are an important factor that drives how we act and behave. Common personal values within a team are the glue connecting team members at a deeper level.

Below, you will find an example of a common personal values assessment of the team. **Team members were asked:** Which of the following values and behaviours most represent who you are?

Personal values	Percentage	Ranking
Teamwork	57%	1
Positive attitude	50%	2
Accountability Honesty	43%	3

Assessment of personal values of the team members (top three ranking)
(Source: Barrett Values Centre)

This example shows that the most common personal value of the team is teamwork. Other important common values are a positive attitude, accountability, and honesty. If someone in the team acts in a manner that goes against an important common value (for example, teamwork), other team members are likely to react highly emotionally, which might (often unconsciously) trigger ineffective behaviours.

Current values indicate how working in the team is experienced at present. This example shows that risk-taking is the most important current value of the team, followed by goals orientation. **Employees were asked:** Which of the following values and behaviours most represent how the team works today?

Current values	Percentage	Ranking
Risk-taking	50%	1
Goals orientation	42%	2
Achievement Adaptability Commitment Cross group collaboration Teamwork	36%	3

Assessment of perceived current values of the team (top three ranking)
(Source: Barrett Values Centre)

Desired values indicate what are perceived as essential values to achieve the highest objectives of the team. This example shows that open communication and teamwork are the most important desired values, followed by empowerment and trust. **Employees were asked:** Which of the following values and behaviours are essential for the team to achieve its highest performance?

Desired values	Percentage	Ranking
Open communication Teamwork	50%	1
Empowerment Trust	43%	2
Accountability Achievement Cross group collaboration Respect	36%	3

Assessment of desired values of the team (top three ranking) (Source: Barrett Values Centre)

The difference between desired and current values indicates relevant **'value jumps'** for the team. In the example below, open communication is the value with the highest difference between desired and current value. Team members also see more empowerment, respect, trust and transparency as essential to achieving its highest objectives. The percentage for personal values gives an indication of the complexity/ease of introducing this value and related behaviour. The higher the percentage, the easier it is to include this value/behaviour in the team.

Values	Current	Desired	Delta	Personal
Open communication	7%	50%	-43%	21%
Empowerment	7%	42%	-36%	21%
Respect	7%	36%	-29%	7%
Trust	14%	43%	-29%	29%
Transparency	7%	29%	-21%	14%

Potential 'value jumps' (top two ranking) (Source: Barrett Values Centre)

The difference between personal and current values indicates **'hot buttons'**, which are possible sources of frustration for team members. In the example below, team members indicate that they wish to see more honesty, integrity, positive attitudes, accountability, and teamwork within the core team. The fact that this is only available to a limited extent creates potential frustrations.

Values	Current	Personal	Delta
Honesty	0%	43%	-43%
Integrity	0%	36%	-36%
Positive attitude	14%	50%	-36%
Accountability	14%	43%	-29%
Teamwork	36%	57%	-21%

Potential hot buttons, sources of frustration (top two ranking) (Source: Barrett Values Centre)

Behaviours to be preserved or changed

The online survey, in-depth interviews and team observation give first indications of team behaviours to be preserved and changed.

During a team intervention, suggestions for team behaviours that should be preserved were:

- I discuss the most important and difficult issues during meetings.
- I keep looking for ways to continuously improve and grow at individual and team level.
- I deliver results.
- I contribute to a fun, high energy and positive atmosphere.

Examples of team behaviours that needed to be changed were:

- I give and accept unprovoked, constructive feedback without taking it personally.
- I push back, and dare to voice when something is not feasible, realistic, or possible (also to upper management).
- I respect different working styles of other team members; when conflict occurs.
- I confront and make sure we deal with the issue before moving on to another subject.

Observations regarding interpersonal dynamics in the team

Below, you will find additional team observations, and a potential explanation of dynamics and tensions. Also, I elaborate on the impact on team performance and coping mechanisms.

Some additional observations

The specific context in which the team operates is characterized by high visibility, expectations and pressure from upper management, a history of successes, and a matrix structure with parallel reporting lines and politics at play at higher levels in the organization. There is diversity in the degree of tension (healthy – unhealthy) and level of manifestation of this tension between specific team members. These tensions might have complicated collaboration and created ineffectiveness and frustration. In this specific case, team members clearly expressed the intention to work together.

Possible explanations regarding tensions and dynamics (hypotheses)

When you bring team members together from different (expert/functional) teams conflicting interests might develop through competition and manifest in (unhealthy) tension or conflict situations. These are normal dynamics.

Also, the survival dilemma (self-preservation) might start to play a role. As explained before, this is the area of tension to protect themselves or their team (identity) versus the necessary collaboration/interaction with others. Anxieties stemming from a lack of recognition or of autonomy/freedom might unconsciously activate defence mechanisms such as micro-management, control, withholding information, and talking about each other instead of with each other.

I assume that there are also several assumptions and misunderstandings about each other (which are insufficiently checked against reality) that confirm and reinforce this behaviour. I also assume that biases play a role: for example, the Horn effect describes how a negative judgement in one instance is likely to result in a negative judgement in the following instance. Confirmation bias is the tendency to search for or interpret information that confirms existing mindsets. These dynamics might be encouraged by an increase in pressure on team members and/or political games at higher levels in the organization.

The impact

Unhealthy tensions between team members might lead to a loss of efficiency (time and energy, reduced productivity) as well as a reduction in morale and motivation. As a result, teams are incited to 'off-tasks'; this means that team members put effort, energy and time into dealing with these negative emotions and frustrations instead of focusing on the primary (business) task of the team.

Coping strategies to improve interpersonal relations

The first step is to become aware of the interpersonal dynamics that support or counteract effective teamwork and to understand their impact. Conducting a reality check on assumptions made about each other as well as increasing trust between team members and developing more empathy (putting yourself in the other person's shoes) are proven tactics to improve interpersonal relations. Other ways to improve rapport between team members are focusing on a strong common mission (rational level), introducing playfulness/fun, and expressing emotions to one another (humanizing the team).

Area 4: Final recommendations

The team evaluation report typically ends with some final recommendations that provide input for discussion, and by defining the objectives of the team coaching session afterwards. The following three recommendations were made in this particular case:

1. Nurture and keep improving the team elements that have been put in place and that currently drive the performance of the team (for example, high overall engagement, recent changes in meeting structure, and a shift towards a more strategic focus).
2. To boost the team towards high performance, we recommend to invest in further building identity/community and taking an even more human, behavioural perspective. Examples of relevant areas of focus are:
   - Increase trust (open dialogue) within the team. Increase psychological safety.
   - Define and align team values and behaviours (how we do things, wanted and unwanted behaviours); change and embed these behaviours.
   - Foster open communication and transparency (challenge, feedback, talk about stress, express emotions).
   - Clarify and implement the team leadership style (top-down/empowerment).
   - Learn to give and accept feedback without taking it personally and becoming defensive.

- Monitor stress levels, discuss this openly and put strategies in place to cope with unhealthy levels of stress.
- Bring the team mission (why) fully to life.

3. The analysis shows the diversity of perception and experience about the functioning of the team in terms of effectiveness, stress, and tension. This means different actions are required to improve performance at team and individual levels.

Never stop investing in trust and psychological safety

Trust is the foundation of effective teams. In my experience, there is always room for improvement in this area. Increasing the level of trust is facilitated by spending time together face to face and by creating a safe space. Team trust typically comes from the vulnerability of members sharing their weaknesses, skill deficiencies, interpersonal shortcomings, mistakes, requests for help and so on. Personality instruments (such as Myers-Briggs, DiSC or Social Styles) are useful tools to help team members understand one another's different preferences and to identify collective strengths and potential blind spots of the team. Making a drawing of themselves and the personal history exercise are tools that provide an opportunity for a quick exchange of personal information.

There's no team without trust.

Over two years, Google conducted 200+ interviews with Googlers and looked at more than 250 attributes of 180+ active Google teams. They were confident that they would find the perfect mix of individual traits and skills necessary for a stellar team. They discovered that they were dead wrong.

They learned that there are five key dynamics that set successful teams apart from other teams at Google:

1. Psychological safety: Can we take risks on this team without feeling insecure or embarrassed?
2. Dependability: Can we count on each other to do high quality work on time?

3. Structure & clarity: Are goals, roles, and execution plans on our team clear?
4. Meaning of work: Are we working on something that is personally important to each of us?
5. Impact of work: Do we fundamentally believe that the work we're doing matters?

Psychological safety was far and away the most important of the five dynamics they found – it underpins the other four.

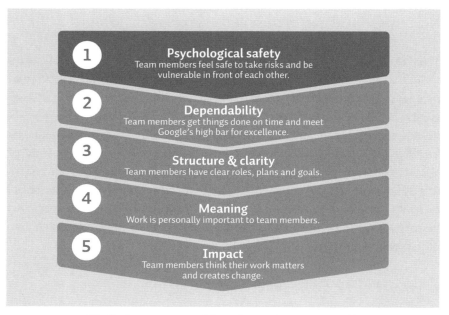

The five keys to a successful Google team (Source: Re:Work)

Psychological safety is defined as 'a belief that one will not be punished or humiliated for speaking up with ideas, questions, concerns, or mistakes'. In a psychologically safe environment, you feel you can stick your neck out without fear of having it cut off. If you do not feel safe in a group, you are likely to keep ideas to yourself and avoid speaking up, even about risks. Furthermore, if mistakes are held against you, you then look to avoid making mistakes and so stop taking risks, rather than making the most of your talents. Research shows that psychological safety is the gateway to high-performing teams.

Google also came up with valuable suggestions on how to increase psychological safety on your own team: Approach conflict as a collaborator, not an adversary; speak human to human; anticipate reactions and plan countermoves; replace blame with curiosity; ask for feedback on delivery and, last but not least, measure it.

TACTIC 3

Conduct team coaching interventions in a safe and reflective setting

---

THE 24-HOUR TEAM COACHING FORMAT

The report with findings resulting from the previous step provides important input for the next step, the team coaching intervention. I often apply the concept of a 24-hour team coaching session that starts at noon and ends at noon the following day. The advantage of this format is that team members can still work on the two days of the session (business continuity) and we create the opportunity to organize an informal team activity during the evening. Moreover, the break overnight (sleeping on it) allows team members to digest the discussions of the first day and they often look at things differently the following morning.

> *Increasing trust, team learning and forming an action plan are the three most common results of team coaching interventions.*

The overall objective of the team coaching intervention is for the team to become more effective at executing the strategy. In particular, to create alignment, trust, and open communication among team members and to get rid of a culture where team members do things their own way, which often results in uncoordinated, conflicting decisions and actions that are not in the best interests of your organization.

The results are often threefold: (1) increased trust, constructive conflict resolution, greater commitment and accountability within the team (2) individual and team contracts (including quick wins) and action plans including setting up follow-up roles to support one another and (3) a learning community whereby team members give feedback whenever they fall back into dysfunctional behavioural patterns.

> *Be flexible about the time needed for discussion of specific topics,*
> *and take the dynamics, emotions, and energy level of the group*
> *into consideration.*

We typically apply the following principles during the 24-hour team coaching session:

- We will invest in creating a safe and reflective space.
- We will maximize the contribution of all participants.
- Although we will design a detailed script for the workshop, we will be flexible about the time needed for discussion of specific topics, and take the dynamics, emotions, and energy level of the group into consideration.
- We will find balance between: (1) minds – hearts/emotions (2) providing information – reflection (3) focus on strengths – focus on weaknesses/development.
- Brain snacks will be integrated in the session to provide fresh, new perspectives, insights and practical tools and to fine-tune energy levels.
- We will make observations on team dynamics, which will be shared with the team during the session and at the debriefing meeting afterwards.

I have learned that in order to create an impactful session it helps to (1) combine the elements of business and human dynamics in a session (2) dance in the moment; leave room for what comes up during the session, allowing deviation from the agenda if this makes sense and (3) contain the anxiety of the team (for a limited time), if they project these feelings.

In my experience, the more structural elements (for example, meetings, team structure, project plans, objectives) that are necessary for a team to be effective are often already in place. The elements for improvement are mostly related to topics like trust, interpersonal dynamics, tensions, transparency, open dialogue, and commitment.

Example of the scope, objectives and results of a team coaching intervention

Building further on the case described and the findings of the previous phase, the scope, objectives and outcomes of the 24-hour coaching session were described as follows.

The scope of the team coaching intervention

- We will focus mainly on the human, behavioural and interpersonal dynamics that increase the effectiveness of the team (less on the structural elements).
- The focus during this intervention will be mainly on the elements that involve and require action from all team members (and less on personal coaching needs or dealing with tensions between some team members).

Key objectives of the team coaching intervention

- To create more awareness of the functioning of the team today in terms of strengths and areas of improvement (based on the analysis done).
- To increase the effectiveness of the team by aligning on the critical areas of improvement, providing practical tools and by starting to practise these (learning).
- To bring the team mission (why) more to life.
- To have fun together.

Results of the team coaching intervention

- Increased trust between team members.
- Clarification and prioritization of desired team behaviour and learning how to put the most critical ones into practice (learning).
- Greater sense of belonging to team (identity).
- Team and individual action plan to move forward.

TRIGGERING, PROVOKING, AND CREATING TIPPING POINTS

It is important to trigger, provoke and create tipping points for change during the session. Tipping points are 'Aha!' moments, sudden moments of insights that make everything click and that result in changes.

> *'When you change the way you look at things, the things you look at change.'* – Max Planck

Manfred Kets de Vries has conceptualized a number of phases in the trajectory of tipping point moments: preparation, incubation, illumination (the tipping point moment), and verification. This deconstruction suggests that preparatory work leading to cognitive, affective, and behavioural reframing of situations is essential to effect tipping point moments. He believes there is a sequence that leads up to 'Aha!' moments, which begins with frustration. When team members become more aware of this frustration and acknowledge it, tipping points are on the rise. Tipping points grow out of thinking and reflection.

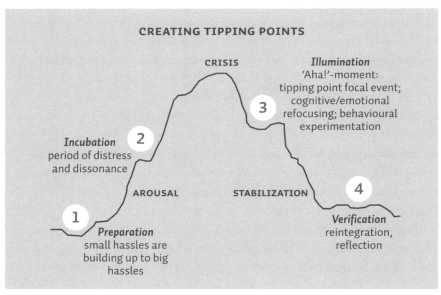

The process of tipping points (Source: Coaching's 'good hour':
Creating tipping points by Manfred Kets de Vries)

LESSONS FROM PAST EXPERIENCES

Below I will share some lessons learned from past experiences that help to reach the objectives of team coaching interventions.

> *Evaluate the intentions of individual team members and their willing-*
> *ness to (really) change.*

Having a good understanding of the intentions of individual team members and of their willingness to change the way they function in the team is crucial in order to build a high-impact team coaching session. In many cases, I found that team members have good intentions for working together but are unconsciously distracted by anxieties, assumptions, beliefs and politics. This leads to silos, which leads to less dialogue, which reinforces silos, creating a negative spiral. In this case, the objective of the session should be on creating awareness about these typical human dynamics. Their impact should be discussed and some mental tools provided to embed this change in mindset and behaviour. If some team members do not have good intentions, the team coaching session needs a different approach.

> *Invest in building an emotionally intelligent team.*

Increasing the level of Emotional Intelligence is often useful in order to reach the objectives of the team coaching session. Through this session, members of the team become more aware of themselves and the interpersonal dynamics between team members. Understanding how their own emotions, beliefs, and values drive their behaviour and impact the effectiveness of the entire team for good or bad are important insights (awareness) to preserve or to change them. This process of awareness starts during the interviews and continues during the session. Examples of quantitative and qualitative tools used to facilitate this are drawing a self-portrait, drawing the current team, personality audits, personal values assessment, and 360 leadership evaluations. In chapter 4, I elaborate in more detail on emotional intelligence and how to develop it.

> *Jointly building a story helps to connect the team at a deeper level and*
> *increases cohesion.*

Building a persuasive story is an exercise that connects team members at a rational and an emotional level. Based on the context, the story can be about different topics, such as the mission, the vision of the team, the change story related to a transformation that is underway, or a report of the results of the coaching session to the teams after the session. I have also found that the creative process of making drawings or the use of images during the story building helps to connect team members at a different level.

Look at improving team effectiveness as an adaptive challenge.

It is critical to identify the type of challenges to change you are facing: adaptive or technical. A technical challenge is defined as one that can be solved by the knowledge of experts, whereas the adaptive challenge requires new learning. When the problem definition, solution, and implementation is clear, Heifetz calls this technical change. Adaptive challenges are characterized by changes in people's priorities, beliefs, habits, and loyalties, and require learning during the process of problem definition and solution.

Improving team effectiveness should most often be seen as an adaptive challenge that requires learning during the process of problem definition and solution. Along with an adaptive challenge goes an adaptive leadership style. In terms of leadership development, Bart had to learn to practise an adaptive leadership style and to develop the ability to deal effectively with ambiguity, uncertainty and tensions, which are unavoidable realities during this journey. In chapter 6, I elaborate in more detail on this concept of adaptive challenges.

Overcoming the fear of conflict is another hot topic in many team coaching sessions.

Better decision making is another hot topic that is often part of the improvement initiative. It is often related to overcoming the fear of conflict within the team. Conflict is about the productive exchange of diverse ideas and opinions in a focused, efficient, and unfiltered way. Without conflict, decision making suffers and relationships among team members stagnate. Some structural or behavioural tactics used are: (1) establish team rules of engagement for acceptable conflict (in terms of behaviours, displays of emotion, language, process) (2) personality assessment to understand specifically how different team members naturally engage in conflict, or (3) the Thomas-Kilmann Instrument (TKI), which helps teams to understand how different strategies for conflict should be employed. The latter, for example, evaluates an individual's behaviour in conflict situations – that is, situations in which the concerns of two people appear to be incompatible. In chapter 4, I elaborate on this model in more detail.

Changing behaviour, or deeply ingrained habits, is not easy to realize but it is feasible.

Changing unwanted behaviour within the team is often an area for improvement. Changing behaviour, or deeply ingrained habits, is not easy to realize but it is feasible. It is important to start small (baby steps) and to start by understanding where the behaviour comes from (personality, beliefs, values), how it impacts the effectiveness of the team and what holds team members back from making the change happen (the competing commitment). A more mental approach is needed to make this happen. Some proven mental tools I use are 'checking assumptions and beliefs', 'the principle of charity', 'the four Toltec agreements' and 'competing commitments':

· The mental tool **'Checking assumptions and beliefs'** allows you to modify and change feelings by means of logical deductive reasoning, instead of allowing your feelings to get the better of you. It allows you to tune in to the inner dialogue, the belief system that is responsible for your feelings and behaviour. In chapter 3, I elaborate further on this mental tool.

· The mental tool **'Principle of charity'** is somewhat related to the previous mental tool and offers a simple methodological prescription for fighting our natural tendency to treat our own interpretations as facts. It relies on the acknowledgement that our mind is a translator and one that is prone to making mistakes. The idea is called the principle of charity: you should try to interpret the statements and actions of people in a way that maximizes the reasonableness of those statements and actions. The underlying assumption is that most of the time people are quite reasonable, and so exercising the principle of charity can mitigate potential misunderstandings. In chapter 3, I elaborate in more detail on this mental tool.

- The mental model **'The four Toltec agreements'** gives inspiration on how to improve the functioning of teams. Don Miguel Ruiz reveals the source of self-limiting beliefs that rob us of joy and create needless suffering. Based on ancient Toltec wisdom, The Four Agreements offer a powerful code to make change in behaviour happen. The four agreements are: 1. Be impeccable with your word. 2.Don't take anything personally. 3. Do not make assumptions. 4. Always do your best.

- The mental tool **'Competing commitments'** is an introspective exercise that helps to better understand the hidden competing commitments that make it hard to change your behaviour. It is about creating awareness about what (unconsciously) blocks you to make the change (immunity to change). In the book *The Real Reason People Won't Change*, Kegan and Lahey show how our individual beliefs, along with the collective mindsets in organizations, combine to create a natural but powerful immunity to change. They assert that change is extremely difficult, be it on the personal or the organizational level, due to hidden competing commitments, sweeping assumptions and ingrained thought patterns that discourage individuals and teams from abandoning the status quo. In chapter 3, I elaborate in more detail on this mental tool.

← PREVIOUS PAGES

Peter's narrative

We are One

Colleagues acknowledge the relationship between their own individuality, their own sovereignty and being able to act as one. When success arrives, they embrace each other and reaffirm symbolically being one, which means they all own the successes.

Summarizing the main points

- **Effective teamwork is identified by many researchers as one of the core practices in high-performing organizations.** The ability to quickly build, deploy, disband, and reform teams is a critical skill for today's organizations.

- **Three HUMAN-centred tactics** that I found to be highly impactful in creating high-performing teams are:

  1. Invest in understanding the human dynamics within the team and its impact on performance.
  2. Never stop investing in trust and psychological safety.
  3. Conduct team coaching interventions in a safe and reflective setting.

- **How much time and effort of team members is sidetracked by emotions, tensions, and conflicts?** All kinds of unconscious human dynamics (such as the survival dilemma) are often a source of ineffectiveness in teams. It is worth understanding these to make sure appropriate, impactful actions for improvement are taken.

- **Improving team effectiveness** is often an adaptive challenge characterized by changes in team member's priorities, beliefs and habits, and requiring learning in the process of problem definition and solution.

- If changes in team behaviour are required, which is often the case, I recommend applying **mental tools** to facilitate these critical shifts.

- **Trust is the foundation of high-performing teams**. In my experience, it is critical to focus on the (good) intentions of team members and their willingness to change. Building emotional intelligence within the team also pays off.

- Throughout the team coaching initiative and especially during the team coaching interventions **tipping points** for changes will be triggered and lead to shifts in critical behaviours.

► How to get started

Identify a team in your organization you are a member of and that scores less than 7 on a scale of 1 to 10 in terms of effectiveness.

Please describe why you gave the team this score.

TACTIC 1
Invest in understanding the human dynamics within the team and its impact on performance

---

► **Some reflections to get started**
- What is the percentage of time/effort (estimate) during which team members are sidetracked from their core functions to deal with emotions, tensions, and conflicts within the team?
- Overall, is the focus of team members more on 'ME' (individual) or 'WE' (common)?
- How do you estimate the willingness and openness of team members to become better as a team?

► **Make a drawing of how you experience the functioning of the team today. After having made the drawing, write down the words that you associate with the drawing.** Reflect on your drawing by asking questions like: What comes to mind? How do I feel when looking at the drawing? What is difficult? Where am I in this drawing?

► **Evaluate the effectiveness of the team.** To better understand the level of potential for improvement of dysfunction in the team, ask yourself the following questions:
- Do team members openly and readily disclose their opinions?
- Are team meetings compelling and productive?
- Does the team come to decisions quickly and avoid getting bogged down by consensus?
- Do team members confront one another about their shortcomings?

- Do team members sacrifice their own interests for the good of the team? *(Source: The Table Group/Lencioni)*

What do you see as key areas for improvement? Trust, handling of conflict, commitment, accountability, result orientation? Anything else?

▶ **Ask yourself more in-depth questions about the functioning of the team.** Think about relevant areas of focus: engagement, pride, energy key drivers and drains, level of stress, values, collaboration, wanted and unwanted behaviours, decision making, team communication …
Some examples of qualitative and quantitative questions:

- What are key areas of strength of the team?
- What are key areas of improvement of the team?
- How would you score their effectiveness on a scale of 1 to 10?
- Which picture comes to mind when you think of the team today?
- How do you feel when you think of the team? (happy, excited, worried, frustrated, scared, sad, angry, surprised)
- If you could change one thing, what would it be?
- What are drivers of pride related to the team?
- What gives/drains energy when you think of the team?
- What are key drivers of stress?

What did you discover about the functioning of the team? Please describe.

TACTIC 2
Never stop investing in trust and psychological safety

▶ **Evaluate the psychological safety in the team.** How would you score the statements below on a scale of 1 (Strongly Disagree) to 5 (Strongly Agree)? Use the statements below as a reference for reflection.
1. When someone makes a mistake in the team, it is never held against him or her. SCORE:_____
2. In the team, it is easy to discuss difficult issues and problems. SCORE:_____
3. In the team, people are rarely rejected for being different. SCORE:_____
4. It is completely safe to take a risk in this team. SCORE:_____

5. It is easy to ask other members of the team for help. SCORE:_____
6. Members of the team value and respect each other's contributions.
   SCORE:_____
   (Source: Amy C. Edmondson, The Fearless Organization Scan)

What did you discover? What do you suggest undertaking to increase the psychological safety in the team?

TACTIC 3
Conduct team coaching interventions in a safe and reflective setting

► **Take a step back and look at your findings. What are topics you suggest addressing during a team coaching intervention?**

Examples of topics are:
- ☐ Team mission, vision, ambitions
- ☐ Interpersonal dynamics
- ☐ The level of trust within the team
- ☐ Team and/or individual objectives
- ☐ Team values and behaviours
- ☐ Changes in behaviour of the team such as decision making, use of time and/or interaction, conflict handling
- ☐ Dealing with stress
- ☐ Dealing with conflicts
- ☐ Team and/or individual action plan
- ☐ Fun /social activity

► **What did you learn? What are you going to do next?**

....
....
....
....
....

Good luck!

'No passion so effectually robs the mind of all its powers of acting and reasoning as fear.'

– Edmund Burke

Introduction and chapter 1: **Key references and interesting reads**

Barrett, B. (2016). *My Team's Level of Trust: Session Leader Guide.* Retrieved from https://www.valuescentre.com/resources

Barrett, R. (2017). *Building a values-driven organization: a whole system approach to cultural transformation.* London: Routledge.

Bird, V. (2017, June 9). Why Teams Matter. Retrieved December 13, 2020, from https://www.belbin.com/resources/blogs/why-teams-matter/

Brewer, M., & Silver, M. (1978). 'Ingroup bias as a function of task characteristics.' *European Journal of Social Psychology* 8, no. 3.

Delizonna, L., Tjan, A., Walker, C., & Renner, S. (2017, August 24). *High-Performing Teams Need Psychological Safety. Here's How to Create It.* Retrieved August 06, 2020, from https://hbr.org/2017/08/high-performing-teams-need-psychological-safety-heres-how-to-create-it

Deloitte (2017). Insights article: *Organizational design: The rise of teams.*

Deloitte, Global Human Capital Trends (2019). *Organizational performance: It's a team sport.*

Edmondson, A. C. (2019). *The fearless organization: Creating psychological safety in the workplace for learning, innovation, and growth.* Hoboken (N.J.): John Wiley & Sons.

Ewenstein, B., Smith, W., & Sologar, A. (2015, July 1). Changing change management. Retrieved December 13, 2020, from https://www.mckinsey.com/featured-insights/leadership/changing-change-management

French, R. B., & Simpson, P. (2010). 'The Work Group: Redressing the balance in Bion's Experiences in Groups'. *Human Relations*, 2010.

Guiette, A., & Vandenbempt, K. (2013). Exploring team mental model dynamics during strategic change implementation in professional service organizations. A sensemaking perspective. *European Management Journal*, 31(6), 728-744.

Heifetz, R., Grashow, A., & Linsky, M. (2009). *The Practice of Adaptive Leadership: Tools and Tactics for Changing Your Organization and the World.* Boston, Massachusetts: Harvard Business School Publishing.

Hellwig, T., Rook, C., Florent-Treacy, E. ,& Kets de Vries, Manfred F. R. (2017). *An Early Warning System for Your Team's Stress Level.*

Retrieved October 22, 2020, from https://hbr.org/2017/04/
an-early-warning-system-for-your-teams-stress-level

Huy, Q. (2016, January 04). Five Reasons Most Companies Fail
at Strategy Execution. Retrieved December 13, 2020,
from https://knowledge.insead.edu/blog/insead-blog/
five-reasons-most-companies-fail-at-strategy-execution-4441

Kegan, R., & Laskow, L. (2001). The Real Reason People Won't Change.
Harvard Business Review, Nov 2001.

Keller, S., Meaney, M. (2017). *High-performing teams: A timeless leadership
topic.* McKinsey Quarterly.

Kets de Vries, Manfred F. R. (2013). Coaching's 'good hour': Creating
tipping points. Coaching: An International Journal of Theory, *Research
and Practice*, 6(2), 152-175. doi:10.1080/17521882.2013.806944

Kets de Vries, Manfred F. R. (2013). The hedgehog effect: *The secrets of
building high performance teams.* San Francisco: Jossey-Bass.

Klimoski R. & Mohammed S. (1994) Team mental model: Construct or
metaphor? *Journal of Management* 20(2): 403.

Lencioni, P. (2012). *The Five Dysfunctions of a Team. A Leadership Fable.*
San Francisco, CA: Jossey- Bass.

Long, S. (2013). *Socioanalytic Methods: Discovering the Hidden in Organisations
and Social Systems*, London: Karnac.

Mohammed S., Klimoski R. & Rentsch J.R. (2000). The measurement
of team mental models: We have no shared schema. *Organizational
Research Methods* 3(2): 123–165.

Palmer, B., & Reed, B. (1971). *An introduction to Organizational Behaviour.*
Retrieved from http://www.grubbinstitute.org.uk

Re:Work – *The five keys to a successful Google team.* (n.d.). Retrieved
August 06, 2020, from https://rework.withgoogle.com/blog/
five-keys-to-a-successful-google-team/

Rice, A. K. (1969). Individual, Group and Inter-Group Processes. *Human
Relations* Vol 22, No 6, p. 565.

Thomas, K. W., & Kilmann, R. H. (2007). *Thomas-Kilmann conflict mode
instrument.* Mountain View, CA: CPP.

Why do most transformations fail? A conversation with Harry Robinson.
(2019, July 10). Retrieved December 13, 2020, from https://www.
mckinsey.com/business-functions/transformation/our-insights/
why-do-most-transformations-fail-a-conversation-with-harry-robinson

CHAPTER 2
Humanizing COLLABORATION across teams

A HUMAN-centred approach to making teams work together effectively

'*Every established order tends to make its own entirely arbitrary system seem entirely natural.*'
– Pierre Bourdieu

**Why don't we get
rid of the silos within
my organization?**

What if the people in my organization work together spontaneously across teams?

Why it matters

In the organizations I have worked in and consulted for over the past 25 years, I experienced the challenges of collaboration and the daily struggles to get rid of silo-working and silo-mentality.

Collaboration between groups is often ineffective. It does not create the intended value and even destroys the organization's value. Missed client opportunities, mistakes, delays, time wasted due to conflict, poor decisions, and a lack of shared learning are examples of drivers of this ineffectiveness.

Additionally, research focusing on the future of the organization of work indicates the emergence of new ecosystems and more horizontal organizations that are based on the critical foundation of effective collaboration.

A story to tell: 'Us' versus 'them'

Victor, head of international expansion of a French company, contacted me to talk about a business challenge he had been facing for some time. I went to see him at his office, and he started to explain the painful situation he was in. His company was founded in France more than a decade ago. As part of the international expansion, Victor had decided to replicate the successful business concept they had developed to the UK, with some adaptations to local needs.

⋮ *Victor's challenges and hopes*

Tension had mounted between the French and UK teams, which manifested in power games, bad-mouthing the other team, strong protectionism within both teams, heavy competition, a strong split between 'them' and 'us', and time wasted on conflict between them. Endless discussions and 'fights to be right' became the default interaction between them. A lot of energy, effort and time went into dealing with the negative energy and frustrations.

Since the start of the expansion, the local UK team had been replaced several times. Victor realized that effective interaction and collaboration with the French team was essential for the success of his new business in the UK. He was quite desperate and wanted to avoid replacing the UK team yet again. This would mean the end of expansion in the UK, and the loss of a great business opportunity. I felt his frustration in every word.

Launching the initiative to deal with silo-working

After the initial briefing, we had several follow-up discussions to create a better understanding of the challenges, the approach to be taken and our roles in this initiative. We agreed on how to approach his challenge and decided to start working together on an initiative to improve the collaboration between the French and UK teams. I was very excited to support him because of the complexity, my curiosity to discover what was really going on (the real issue), and the value I could bring by combining my business and psychological expertise.

Based on similar project experiences to improve collaboration between teams and the research I did at INSEAD on this subject, I felt well equipped to deal with the complex nature of inter-group collaboration. I was familiar with the hidden emotional motives and human dynamics between teams that often lead to an (unconscious) focus on beating the other team (competition) rather than maximizing the value of the overall organization. It is often forgotten that this competition can significantly decrease efficiency and effectiveness.

As a next step, we agreed on the people to be involved in one-on-one in-depth interviews. We selected nine people from different functional areas representing the teams: four members of the UK team and five of the French team.

After an email exchange with the co-sponsor in the UK, we agreed on the final list of participants, and sent out emails to the participants with some context about the initiative we were going to launch.

Exploring the essence of the collaborative experience

I started to conduct interviews in France first. I met each of the five selected team members separately for two hours in a quiet place in their office. No preparation was required from the participant and the session was taped to maximize my attention.

At the beginning of each session, I set the context and objectives of the interview and we clarified and agreed on the confidentiality rules. I took some time to build trust with each of them and to create a safe and reflective space. Then we started the creative process. I asked the participant to draw a picture of their experience of the interaction between the French and UK teams. Based on past experiences, I knew that these drawings would provide an enormous amount of rich data about conscious and unconscious experiences that team members have during this collaboration.

I gave guidelines and instructions to make sure they felt comfortable drawing, such as 'There is no right or wrong', 'Don't think too much and follow your gut feel', 'Enjoy and have fun'.

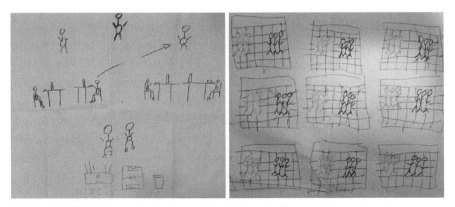

Examples of two drawings representing the collaboration between the French and UK teams

Afterwards, I asked the team member to present me their drawing and we jointly explored it in detail. I brought my knowledge of free associations, positioning of people in the drawing, metaphors and aspects of sequence, size, detailing, symmetry, placement, and motion into the discussion. I asked questions like: Where are you in the story? How do you feel when looking at the drawing? What is difficult? What comes to mind? My objective was to create data from the point of view of each team member (existing and ideal internal mental representation), their view on the other group (inter-group projections) and their view on how they think the other group sees them (introjections). We closed each session with a wrap-up: I thanked them for the discussion and gave them the space to bring up any final questions or reflections.

The drawings on page 81 revealed that conflicts and 'fights to be right' between the French and UK teams occurred regularly and that the French team took over from the UK team and intervened at the last minute to rescue them.

> *Endless discussions and 'fights to be right' seemed to be the default way to interact between the teams*

I decided to use the first two face-to-face sessions as pilots, to allow me to fine-tune my approach, as I found that the use of silence, and of metaphors was powerful. I personally tried to be even more open-minded during the interviews – to be without memory, desire, or understanding. I also decided to add a follow-up call a week after each face-to-face interview. As the interviews were rather intense and overwhelming for them, I wanted to find out if new insights and reflections might have come to mind after a week of digestion, which was the case.

In parallel with the interviews, I launched a survey to all members of the teams to collect more quantitative information about the effectiveness of the collaboration. The focus was on the underlying values, the level of trust between the teams and the quality of relationships and communication between them.

At the UK office, I applied the same approach.

Afterwards, I analyzed the data I had collected from the surveys and inter-views. I listened to the recordings, and consolidated and integrated all the data. This related to their thoughts, feelings, behaviours, assumptions, values, memories, fantasies, and anxieties. I also collected data related to interpersonal dynamics within and between the teams.

Decoding the human dynamics within and between the teams

I noted key points and reflections and associations that came to my mind and used myself as an instrument. As I was doing this, an image came to me – the image of a foster child. I saw two couples living on different sides of the ocean; one couple has a child, the other does not. Every year the natural parents send their child by boat to the other couple, the foster parents. The natural parents love their child dearly and find it tough to let go and to share the child. They are also very anxious about the well-being of their child. Previously, the natural parents had found that the foster parents treated the child like any other child, with no special care and little love. Often, the natural parents crossed the ocean in a speed boat to rescue the child. Today, the natural parents feel that the foster parents have good intentions. The foster parents love the child but realize that they will never be able to love the child as much as the natural parents do.

As a next step, I developed a working note with a summary of my findings. The objective of this note was not to give answers or an explanation of the problems but as an invitation to create awareness about the situation from a different perspective. Examples of repeating behavioural patterns I observed between the teams were: the reflex to escalate issues in the hierarchy within their own team, 'fights to be right', French team takes over at the last minute, UK ideas are rejected, decisions are over-ruled by the French team, and so on. I was interested to better understand what drove these repeating behavioural patterns and to make their impact explicit.

A working note described the repeating behavioural patterns observed between the teams and the impact on its performance

A key hypothesis I made was that the French team (unconsciously) did not give full authority to the UK team to do the work because they are afraid of being abused or destroyed (threat to identity), and afraid to lose control, self-esteem and recognition. On the other hand, a key anxiety of the UK team was related to extreme dependency on the French team, not being included (identity) and the lack of recognition. It also became clear that the aftermath of past bad experience was still present in the stories told and that the tension between the teams concentrated mainly around power and identity.

Afterwards, I brought the members of both teams together in a session to discuss and explore my findings and my working hypotheses on the dynamics between the teams. The more quantitative survey results were also integrated into the discussion. Some of the issues revealed were that the frequency, timeliness, and accuracy of communication and the perceived level of trust between the teams were rather low.

⋮ *Bringing findings back to the teams in a safe and reflective space*

I started shifting focus onto the impact of these dynamics and, ultimately, we jointly defined the supporting structure required to facilitate the transition towards more effective collaboration.

The session was designed to offer hunches on the initial working hypotheses. I paid attention to the way I presented the working note as it could have been perceived merely as an interpretation from the facilitator, with resulting disengagement of the team. Co-creation of meaning was a must. I continued working with drawings to enhance the team's capacity to think creatively together and, in turn, to work creatively in their primary roles. I also took the time at the beginning of the session to create a safe, reflective space and the right container to allow them to explore collaboration at the conscious and emotional, unconscious levels.

I was the comforter and – temporarily – contained the anxieties stirred up by the uncertainty and ambiguity of the process. I also applied a combination of two models of consulting, the 'expert model' and the 'reflective model'. This made sense because the problem required my expertise in reaching a solution, and the team would learn more effectively through joint exploration.

Throughout and after the session I observed changes in the language of the participants (use of more 'we'), which were important indicators of tipping points – shifts in awareness leading to changes in behaviour.

Based on this critical workshop, we started to define and implement some structural strategies with a focus on governance, decision making (matrix) between the teams, meeting structure, and the way to exchange knowledge. We also aligned on and made the common objectives for both teams (at organizational level) very explicit. We complemented this with behavioural strategies at an individual level (intrapersonal), between people (interpersonal), within teams (intrateam) and between teams (inter-team). Some mental tools were also introduced within the teams to support more effective interaction and collaboration.

Structural and behavioural strategies to make it work this time

Victor and I discussed his role as a leader extensively, both in this initiative and in the transition to be made. It was important to look at it as an adaptive challenge (and not as a technical problem), which is characterized by changes in people's priorities, beliefs, habits, and loyalties, and requires learning in the process of problem definition and solution.

I continued following up, coaching them during the implementation of these new strategies, then finally disengaged to make them self-reliant. To reinforce and embed the change, the focus remained heavily on monitoring the quality of the communication and relationship, and the level of trust between both teams and openness of constructive dialogue.

By applying human-centred approaches, we increased the effectiveness of the collaboration between the French and UK teams and managed to shift the focus and energy back to the core business activities.

Three HUMAN-centred tactics

In the section below I want to share three human-centred tactics that I experienced as highly impactful in increasing the effectiveness of the collaboration across teams:

1. Invest in decoding the human dynamics in the collaborative.
2. Strengthen the foundation of trust and facilitate open dialogue.
3. Put the real issues on the table before taking action.

Below I elaborate on each of the three human-centred tactics in more detail.

TACTIC 1
Invest in decoding the human dynamics in the collaborative

THE COMPLEX NATURE OF COLLABORATION

Although the start of a collaboration can be conscious and rational, the process is often influenced by hidden, emotional and unconscious motives and human dynamics. The fact that these dynamics change easily contributes to the complex nature of a collaboration.

Survival as a team often becomes the primary focus

The survival of any system – whether individual or group – depends on the interactions with its environment. This creates the dilemma: How can I maintain a sense of identity and continuity as a person or group (leading to preservation and isolation), and at the same time contribute to, and receive from others (leading to connection and integration)?

There are two kinds of models for how we regulate behaviours. The first kind is directed towards securing our survival in the face of threatening disintegration, to avoid confronting what we feel are intolerable demands on us. In this case, our behaviour is redirected to the immediate task of defending ourselves and the application of defence mechanisms (such as denial, repression, rationalization). These social defences often lead to a loss of efficiency (time and energy, reduced productivity) as well as a reduction in morale and motivation. As a result, teams are incited to 'off-tasks'; this means that team members devote effort, energy and time towards dealing with these negative emotions and frustrations instead of focusing on the primary (business) task of the collaboration. In the second kind of mental activity, we organize our behaviour, not to discharge painful feelings that threaten us, but to achieve objectives through rational investigation and work.

In the story I told above, I strongly sensed the (survival) dilemma within the French team, the tension between the need to interact (which drives behaviour towards connection and collaboration) and the need to protect their identity (which drives behaviour towards isolation). When looking at the effectiveness of collaboration between the teams, I experienced the importance of getting a good sense of the focus on securing the 'me' versus 'we' of both teams and the competition between them. It significantly influenced the behaviours of the teams.

Typical behaviours between and within competing groups

During a collaboration, conflicting interests might develop through competition into overt social conflict. You might recognize some of the examples below of behavioural patterns between and within competing groups.

Examples of human dynamics between (competing) groups:

- ☐ Each group begins to see the other group as an enemy.
- ☐ Each group begins to experience distortions of perception – it tends to perceive only the best part of itself, denying its weaknesses, and tends to see only the worst parts of the other group, denying their strengths.
- ☐ Hostility towards the other group increases while interaction and communication with the other group decreases.
- ☐ During interaction, group members tend to listen only for information that supports their own position and stereotype.

Examples of human dynamics within groups:

- ☐ Each group becomes more closely knit and elicits greater loyalty from its members; members close ranks and bury some of their internal differences.
- ☐ The group climate changes from informal, casual and playful to work and task oriented; concerns about members' psychological needs decline while concerns about task accomplishment increase.
- ☐ Leadership patterns tend to change from more democratic towards more autocratic; the group becomes more willing to tolerate autocratic leadership.
- ☐ Each group becomes more highly structured and organized.
- ☐ Each group demands more loyalty and conformity from its members in order to be able to present a 'solid front'.

Beating the competition rather than maximizing the organization's value

In his research, Caruso argues that there are three key barriers to effective coordination and information sharing across teams: (1) inter-group bias (2) the basic need for self-esteem and (3) group territoriality.

(1) Inter-group bias is the systematic tendency to unfairly treat one's own group or its members better than a non-membership group or its members.

(2) The basic need for self-esteem encourages members of affected groups to use such distinctions to their advantage – that is, to set themselves apart from others in ways that enhance their image and reputation. Therefore, group members are likely to behave in ways that promote a favourable reputation for their own group relative to other groups, or 'positive distinctiveness'.

(3) Group territoriality – organizational boundaries to distinguish groups from one another and to identify the territory each will occupy within the organization – is another key barrier to effective coordination and information sharing across teams as it might afford group members a sense of psychological ownership or to claim feelings of possessiveness and attachment towards territorial objects. They may begin to see themselves as the sole rightful performers of certain tasks or possessors of certain knowledge, and then hold themselves to those expectations by restricting their activities and information exchange to in-group members.

In summary, the goal for group members becomes to beat the competition rather than maximizing value, which discourages cooperative activity.

EXPLORING 'COLLABORATION-IN-THE-MIND', THE ESSENCE OF THE COLLABORATION

Actors in a collaborative often create a subjective, emotional reality of the collaboration, and build up self-constructed images based on previous experiences, guesswork, internal mental models of their own group and perception of the other group. These self-constructed images influence how individuals and teams behave in a collaborative. The resulting dynamics either help or hinder how effectively they perform tasks together.

Understanding the subjective, emotional reality of the collaboration is key

Within the study of cognitive psychology, 'mental map' is a term used to describe the way we make sense of our world, or our perception of reality. It represents how we perceive and interpret the world that operates around us at the cognitive and emotional level. When an actual event is experienced within this model, the individual can interpret it without undue anxiety or embarrassment. If it turns out to be different from what he or she expected, the individual is faced with the choice of withdrawal, adaptation, or modification.

Teams also have mental maps, the shared, organized understanding and mental representation of knowledge about key elements of the team's relevant environment. Members of a group not only have a shared mental map of its internal relationships, but also of other groups. They have partly or wholly shared ideas of other groups, which may be lumped together into an object of suspicious thought simply as 'them', or they may be conceived individually and more realistically.

I found that discovering and understanding individual and mental maps as well as the interpersonal and inter-group dynamics and relations is an imperative to improving and transitioning towards more effective collaboration.

It is important to understand the essence of the collaborative experience of both parties and to collect and analyze data on 'what' they experienced and 'how' they experienced it. I call this 'Collaboration-in-the-mind'.

> *Understanding 'Collaboration-in-the-mind' is an imperative to becoming more effective*

As shown in the figure below 'Collaboration-in-the-mind' includes internal mental representation of the own group in a collaborative (perception of self), inter-group projections (perception of the other group) and inter-group introjections (perception of how the other group might see themselves).

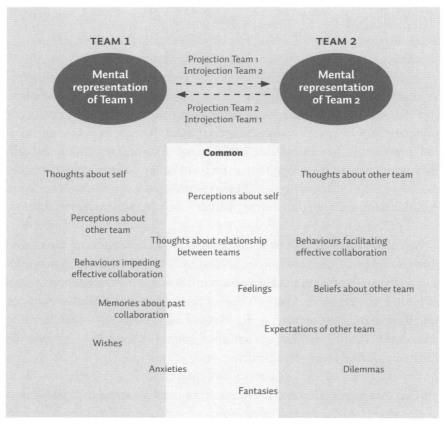

Visualization of the concept 'Collaboration-in-the-mind'

In the story I told earlier, interviews with team members revealed insightful stories about the collaboration. Based on the story of the two teams, I found examples of statements, sentences, and quotes that I analyzed in order to understand how team members from the French team experienced the collaboration. It gave a good sense of the 'Collaboration-in-the-mind' of the French team.

Below you find examples of associations I discovered that reveal 'Collaboration-in-the-mind'.

EXAMPLES OF THOUGHTS, FEELINGS, AND BEHAVIOURS **EXPRESSED BY FRENCH TEAM MEMBERS ABOUT THE COLLABORATION:**

- When the UK and French team meet in person (which happens a few times each year), the collaboration is perceived as positive and productive. When the teams are back in their respective home countries and offices, the collaboration is perceived as less positive and more difficult and challenging.
- Conflicts and 'fights to be right' between the French and UK teams occur regularly.
- Issues between counterparts of both teams are sometimes escalated to the higher levels in their team hierarchies and discussions about the issue and expression of frustration happen within each of the teams.
- The French team takes over from the UK team and intervenes at the last minute to rescue them.
- The French team is frustrated in situations where agreements have been made between the French and UK teams and afterwards the UK team deviates from what has been agreed, and goes its own way.

EXAMPLES OF BELIEFS, ASSUMPTIONS AND VALUES **EXPRESSED**
BY THE FRENCH TEAM ABOUT THEMSELVES:

- We are winners and have proven ourselves.
- We have the final word to protect the unique business event concept of our company.
- We are passionate, put our heart and soul into the company ('It's our baby') and go the extra mile.
- We are goal oriented, specific, detailed in our approach and execution, and can make things happen.
- Important values are: teamwork, taking care of each other, emphasis on the team over the individual, friendship, taking responsibility, and trust.

EXAMPLES OF BELIEFS, ASSUMPTIONS AND VALUES **EXPRESSED**
BY THE FRENCH TEAM ABOUT THE UK TEAM:

- They have a lot of pride and like to shine, get exposure, and show off.
- They like to do things the way they want them done.
- They still have to prove themselves and have a lot to do to reach the level of experience of the French team.
- The expression 'I'm on it' is used, but this does not seem to be the case from our perspective. Sometimes they stay high level and do not always fill in the details.
- They often miss deadlines, they are vague and inefficient.
- In some cases, they are more focused at the individual level than at the team level and take a hierarchical perspective (for example, in a crisis, some people did not help because they did not see it as their role).
- Lack of transparency; hidden agendas at times.
- They do not put the same passion, heart and soul into the company.

- Be passionate, put your heart and soul into the project, 'love and take care of our baby' and go the extra mile.
- Empathize with our unique business event concept.
- Work for us to implement our vision.
- Be grateful for the unique product you can roll out in your country.
- Follow, listen, do not show off.
- Work independently.
- Similar insights were created from a UK team perspective. As a next step, I created a working note that gave a summary of the key findings and hypotheses on the human dynamics within and between the teams.

Measuring values and the quality of the relationships and communication

Qualitative methods like drawing provide an enormous amount of rich data about the experience during a collaboration. Its power resides in its capacity to give simple expression to complex feelings and to give ideas about the collaboration. Based on my experience, it makes sense to complement this qualitative approach with quantitative methods that provide additional insights about the effectiveness of a collaboration: Values assessment and Relational Coordination Index are two examples of quantitative methods that I often apply in the initiatives to increase the effectiveness of a collaboration.

Discover the 'glue' between teams

Understanding underlying values of team members in a collaborative gives interesting insights about the 'glue' connecting team members at a deeper level, potential sources of frustration between teams (so called 'hot buttons') and how the collaboration can reach its highest effectiveness.

Personal values reflect what is important to us. They are a shorthand way of describing our individual motivations. Together with our beliefs, they are an important factor that drives how we act and behave. Common personal values are the 'glue' connecting team members at a deeper level. Below you will find an example of the common personal values assessment of the two collaborating teams. **The question all team members were asked was:** Which of the following values and behaviours most represent who you are? An example of the results follows below.

Common Personal Values	Percentage	Ranking
Achievement	67%	1
Commitment	67%	1
Entrepreneurial	67%	1

Assessment of common personal values (highest scores) (Source: Barrett Values Centre)

I learned that putting the focus on common personal values creates positive energy within the collaborative. The data also shows that if a team member acts in a manner that goes against an important common value (for example, achievement), others will most probably react very emotionally. This might trigger (often unconsciously) ineffective behaviours in the collaborative.

Identify the critical shifts in values and behaviours to be made

Current values indicate how the collaboration between teams is perceived and experienced today. **The question is:** Which of the following values and behaviours most represent how the collaborative currently operates?

You will find an example of the perceived current values assessment opposite. The current collaboration is mainly experienced as confusing and bureaucratic (both are potential limiting values/behaviours). Other potential limiting values/behaviours experienced today are internal competition, empire building and hierarchy. The positive values/behaviours experienced today are commitment, shared vision, creativity and patience.

Current Values	Percentage	Ranking
Confusion	67%	1
Bureaucracy	67%	1
Commitment	33%	2
Internal Competition	33%	2
Shared Vision	33%	2
Creativity	33%	2
Empire Building	33%	2
Hierarchy	33%	2
Patience	33%	2

Assessment of current values of the collaboration (top two ranking)
(Source: Barrett Values Centre)

Desired values indicate what are perceived as essential values/behaviours to achieve the highest objectives of the team. **The question asked of all team members was:** Which of the following values and behaviours are essential for the collaboration to achieve its highest performance?

The difference between desired and current values provides insights on the values to focus on in order to make the collaboration more effective. They are a great starting point in defining critical shifts in behaviours to be made between the teams. In chapter 3 (Humanizing culture shifts) the way to work with personal, current and desired values and behaviours is elaborated on in more in detail.

Understand the quality of the relationship and communication between the teams

In order to improve the collaboration between teams, it is essential to understand the quality of relationships and communication between them. The Relational Coordination Theory (developed by Relational Coordination Analytics) measures the quality of relationships and communication involved in the coordination of work and measures seven different dimensions:

1. Frequent Communication
2. Timely Communication
3. Accurate Communication
4. Problem-solving Communication
5. Shared Goals
6. Shared Knowledge
7. Mutual Respect

Each dimension is measured on a five-point scale. Relational coordination is an equally weighted average of all seven dimensions. Asking the UK and French team members to complete the questionnaire below helped me to get insights about the strengths and weaknesses of the collaboration.

Statement	Dimension	Score*
Quality of communication		
We frequently communicate with other team members about topics that matter to both of us	Frequent communication	
We communicate with other team members in a timely way about topics that matter to both of us	Timely communciation	
We communicate accurately with other team members about topics that matter to both of us	Accurate communication	
When a problem occurs that involves the other team, we work together to solve the problem	Problem-solving communication	
Quality of relationship		
We share common goals across the teams	Shared goals	
We know about each other's work (other team)	Shared knowledge	
We respect each other's work (other team)	Mutual respect	

* 1 Strongly disagree – 2 Disagree – 3 Neutral – 4 Agree – 5 Strongly agree

Questionnaire to evaluate the quality of the relationship and communication
(Source: RC Analytics)

TACTIC 2
Strengthen the foundation of trust and facilitate open dialogue

Trust lies at the heart of effective collaboration. Absence of trust in a collaborative occurs when team members of a team are reluctant to be vulnerable with members of the other team, and are thus unwilling to admit their mistakes, acknowledge their weaknesses or ask for help. Without a certain comfort level among team members in the different teams, a foundation of trust is impossible.

Asking team members to complete the questionnaire below allows you to start getting insights about the level of trust between them.

Statement	Score*
Team members admit their mistakes to members of the other team	
Team members acknowledge their weaknesses to members of the other team	
Team members ask for help without hesitation to members of the other team	
Team members acknowledge and tap into the other team's skills and expertise	
Team members willingly apologize to members of the other team	
Team members are unguarded and genuine with members of the other team	
Team members can comfortably discuss their personal lives with members of the other team	

*1 Strongly disagree – 2 Disagree – 3 Neutral – 4 Agree – 5 Strongly agree

Questionnaire to evaluate the level of trust between the teams
(Source: The Table Group/Lencioni)

Let us go back to the story. Although trust was perceived as a key value within the French team, the lack of trust between both teams lurked beneath the surface of the discussions. Although improvement in the level of trust with the current UK team had been expressed, elements like a lack of transparency and openness, and especially a lack of skills, knowledge and performance, were mentioned during the discussions (see figure opposite: Barrett's Trust Matrix).

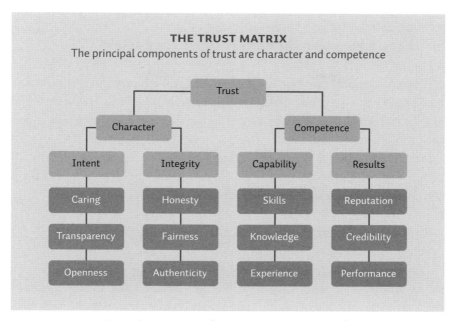

THE TRUST MATRIX
The principal components of trust are character and competence

Trust

Character — Competence

Intent — Integrity — Capability — Results

Caring — Honesty — Skills — Reputation

Transparency — Fairness — Knowledge — Credibility

Openness — Authenticity — Experience — Performance

Barrett's Trust Matrix (Source: Barrett Values Centre)

I assumed that differences in values and perceived character and competence of the UK team fed low trust levels. This low level of trust might have fed the anxiety of being abused and/or destroyed and might ultimately have activated individual and social defence mechanisms as coping mechanisms. Based on the discussion, the trust level from the UK team towards the French team was much higher and was based on French capabilities and results. The perceptions around fairness, transparency and openness might have been elements that were reducing the level of trust towards the French team.

Put the real issues on the table before taking action

Heifetz argues there are two types of challenges: adaptive and technical. A technical challenge is defined as one that can be solved by the knowledge of experts, whereas the adaptive challenge requires new learning. When the problem definition, solution, and implementation is clear, Heifetz calls this technical change. Adaptive challenges are characterized by changes in people's priorities, beliefs, habits, and loyalties, and require learning during the process of problem definition and solution.

Challenges related to inter-group collaboration are often treated solely as technical challenges

Interventions to improve collaboration often do not tackle the root cause of the dysfunctional behaviour but simply fix its manifestations. Challenges related to inter-group collaboration are often treated solely as technical challenges that can be resolved through the application of authoritative expertise, structures and procedures. In this case, the adaptive challenge perspective is not considered. When a more adaptive perspective is taken, the focus is often solely on interpersonal dynamics and interventions like team-building sessions, which often create artificial bonds. An increase in cooperation between those departments by creation of one or several teams composed of people from different departments is another naive belief that is prevalent. I believe that a combined technical and adaptive approach to increase the effectiveness of a collaboration pays off.

Let us bring this back to the story I told earlier. After the creation of the understanding of the essence of the collaborative, I brought both teams together in a working session. The objective was to explore findings, working hypotheses and dynamics. During this session, I also started to shift focus to the impact of these dynamics.

Sharing hypotheses on the dynamics. I wonder if ...

I created a working note that gave a summary of the key findings and hypotheses on the human dynamics within and between the teams. Also, the more quantitative measures on values and the quality of relationships and communication were shared with the teams. I did not position this note as answers or explanations of the problems but as an invitation to the teams to think about the situation from a different perspective.

To illustrate, the four hypotheses on dynamics I shared with the UK and French teams related to the dynamics of the French team were:

- **Hypothesis 1**: I wonder if the French team (unconsciously) did not give full authority to the UK team to do the work because they are afraid that they will be abused or destroyed (threat to identity), or lose control, self-esteem and recognition. This might also be the reason they did not formalize and clarify roles and decision-making processes, instead providing support on a rather ad-hoc, last-minute basis. I assume that the past bad experiences have created a low level of trust, which might have increased their anxieties. In other words, might there be a systematic, unconscious attempt to exclude or isolate the UK team?

- **Hypothesis 2**: Several signs lead to the identification of social defences: rigidity ('we have always done it this way') and splitting ('we are trying to achieve the business event, but they keep complicating our life and making it impossible'). There was also extra focus on needing more information and adding more checks, more checklists, more approvals.

- **Hypothesis 3**: I wonder if within the French team, defence mechanisms were activated like passive aggression (procrastination of support).

- **Hypothesis 4**: I wonder if the French team had a basic shared fantasy, as if there is an enemy (UK team), from which they require a defence or escape. This dynamic is also called fight/flight and is a projection of their own hostile feelings onto the UK team, a splitting of the world into good and bad. These fantasies might have been strengthened through the past bad experiences.

The hypotheses on the dynamics of the UK team were also shared during this session.

I continued working with drawings to enhance their capacity to think creatively together and to increase the capacity for creative work. I also took time at the beginning of the session to create a safe, reflective space, allowing the team to engage in the exploration of the collaboration at conscious and emotional, unconscious levels. During working sessions, I am often the comforter and – temporarily – contain the anxieties stirred up by the uncertainty and ambiguity of the process. I also apply a combination of two models of consulting, the 'expert model' and the 'reflective model'. This makes sense because of the increase in complexity and knowledge required to solve the problem and the focus on learning through joint exploration.

Creating a safe and reflective space

I have learned that engaging in creative play as playfulness (not being completely serious) contributes to the emergence of transitional processes to work through difficult aspects of change.

We also discussed the key role leaders play in the transition towards more effective collaboration. An adaptive leadership style (rather than technical) is essential to make it work. Leading collaborative processes requires leadership to be able to face a lot of ambiguity, uncertainty, and tensions without falling into the position of judging others. Leading collaboration involves creating conditions for the different parties to come to a common problem definition and strategy to deal with it.

Creating awareness, triggering tipping points

An important objective of the whole exercise (from the start) was to trigger, provoke and create tipping points for change. Tipping points are 'Aha!' moments, sudden moments of insights that make everything click and result in changes. Throughout the session I observed changes in the language of the participants (such as the use of more 'we'), which are important indicators of tipping points, shifts in awareness that ultimately lead to changes in behaviour.

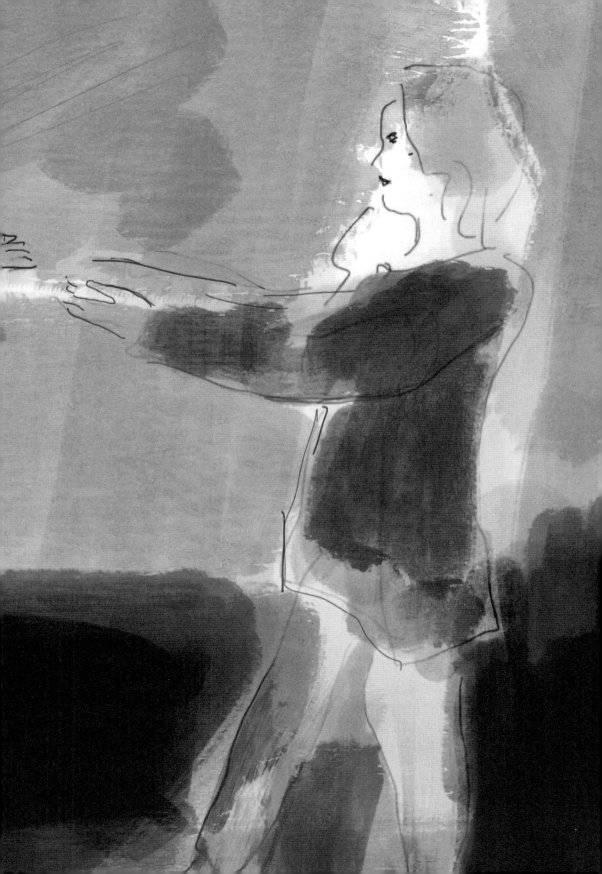

← PREVIOUS PAGES

Peter's narrative

Trust and Transparency

Two individuals seek a new beginning,
to trust each other and to be transparent.
The figure on the far left does not know
herself and therefore can't cross the bridge
with the others. She is encouraging her
team colleague to move away. The pattern
of light and dark on the wall is a visual
representation of transparency.

Summarizing the main points

*Making people in the organization work together spontaneously
across teams*

- **Collaboration across teams is often ineffective.** It does not create the intended value and even destroys the organization's value. Moreover, research focusing on the future of organization of work indicates the emergence of new ecosystems and more horizontal organizations that are based on the critical foundation of effective collaboration.

- **Collaboration is a highly complex phenomenon.** Although the start of a collaboration can be conscious and rational, the process is often influenced by hidden, emotional and unconscious motives and human dynamics. The survival as a team often becomes the primary focus of the team, beating the other team (competition) rather than maximizing the organization's value.

- **Three HUMAN-centred tactics** that I found to be highly impactful to increase the effectiveness of the collaboration between teams are:

  1. Invest in decoding the human dynamics in the collaborative.
  2. Strengthen the foundation of trust and facilitate open dialogue.
  3. Put the real issues on the table.

- Understanding the **'Collaboration-in-the-mind'**, the emotional subjective reality of the collaboration is an imperative for becoming more effective.

- **I recommend applying a combined quantitative and qualitative approach to explore the essence of the collaborative experience.** Using drawings combined with more quantitative methods that evaluate underlying values and the quality of relationships and communication between the teams pays off.

- Presenting and discussing the (mostly hidden) human dynamics, why they might happen (hypotheses) and their impact on performance is an essential step in any initiative to improve collaboration. When done in a safe and reflective setting, **tipping points** for change could happen.

- **The plan to improve collaboration mostly combines structural and behavioural tactics.**

- **As a leader, you play a key role in the transition towards more effective collaboration.** Leading collaborative processes requires an adaptive leadership style and the ability to face ambiguity, uncertainty, and tensions without falling into the position of judging others.

► How to get started

Identify an example of a critical collaboration (internally in your organization or with a partner in your ecosystem/network) you are currently part of, which is in great need of improvement.

► **How would you score the effectiveness of the collaboration on a scale from 0 to 10?**

► **How would you describe the key challenge(s) of this collaborative? What is the impact of these challenges on the performance of your organization?**
Think of drivers of ineffectiveness like missed client opportunities, mistakes, delays, time wasted due to conflict, poor decisions, lack of shared learning and so on.

► **What do you hope will happen?**
Please describe.

TACTIC 1
Invest in decoding the human dynamics in the collaborative

► **Make a drawing of how you experience the collaboration and interaction between the teams today.** After having made the drawing, write down the words that you associate with the drawing. Reflect on your drawing by asking questions like: What comes to mind? How do I feel when looking at the drawing? What is difficult? Where am I in this drawing?

▶ **Do you recognize some of the typical behaviours between the groups?** Please use the list below as a reference for reflection. Examples of dynamics between (competing) groups:

- ☐ Each group begins to see the other group as the enemy.
- ☐ Each group begins to experience distortions of perception – it tends to perceive only the best part of itself, denying its weaknesses, and tends to see only the worst parts of the other group, denying their strengths.
- ☐ Hostility towards the other group increases while interaction and communication with the other group decreases.
- ☐ During interaction, group members tend to listen only for information that supports their own position and stereotypes.

What did you discover about the collaboration? Please describe.

▶ **How would you describe the effectiveness of a collaboration in terms of the quality of relationships and communication between the teams?**
Score the statements below on a scale from 1 (Strongly Disagree) to 5 (Strongly Agree)

1. We frequently communicate with other team members about topics that matter to us all. SCORE:_____
2. We communicate with other team members in a timely way about topics that matter to us all. SCORE:_____
3. We communicate accurately with other team members about topics that matter to us all. SCORE:_____
4. When a problem that involves the other team occurs, we work together to solve the problem. SCORE:_____
5. We share common goals across the teams. SCORE:_____
6. We know about each other's work (other team). SCORE:_____
7. We respect each other's work (other team). SCORE:_____
   (*Source: Relational Coordination Analytics*)

What did you discover about the collaboration? Please describe.

HUMANIZING STRATEGY

TACTIC 2
Strengthen the foundation of trust and facilitate open dialogue

▶ **What are your suggestions for strengthening the foundation of trust between the teams?**
The trust between the teams will increase if team members:

☐ Let go of grudges
☐ Admit their mistakes
☐ Reduce the amount of gossiping
☐ Spend more time together
☐ Get to know one another on a personal level
☐ Are more forthright with information
☐ Readily apologize
☐ Share professional failures and successes
☐ Give credit where credit is due
☐ Understand each other's working style
(Source: The Table Group/Lencioni)

What did you discover about the collaboration? Please describe.

TACTIC 3
Put the real issues on the table before taking action

▶ **Take a step back and define the key insights you discovered about the collaboration.**
What do you see? What comes to mind? What did you discover? What are your hypotheses (I wonder if ... happens, because of ...)?

▶ **Building your improvement plan: What are the structural and behavioural actions you suggest taking?**

▶ **What did you learn? What are you going to do next?**

....

....

....

....

....

Good luck!

'Everything that irritates us
about others can lead us to an
understanding of ourselves.'
– Carl Jung

Chapter 2: **Key references and interesting reads**

Barrett, B. (2016). *My Team's Level of Trust: Session Leader Guide*. Retrieved from https://www.valuescentre.com/resources

Barrett, R. (2017). *Building a values-driven organization: a whole system approach to cultural transformation*. London: Routledge.

Beech, N., & Huxham, C. (2003). Cycles of Identity Formation in Interorganizational Collaborations. *International Studies Of Management & Organization*, 33(3), 28-52.

Billig, M., & Tajfel, H. (1973). Social categorization and similarity in inter-group behaviour. *European Journal of Social Psychology*, Vol. 3(1), 27-52.

Caruso, H. M., Rogers, T., & Bazerman, M. (2009). *Boundaries Need Not Be Barriers: Leading and Creating Collaboration in Decentralized Organizations. Crossing the Divide: Inter-group Leadership in a World of Difference*. Harvard Business School Press, T. Pittinsky Edition.

Gittell, J. H., Seidner, R., & Wimbush, J. (2010). A Relational Model of How High-Performance Work Systems Work. *Organization Science*, 21(2), 490-506. doi:10.1287/orsc.1090.0446.

Gladwell, M. (2015). *The tipping point: How little things can make a big difference*. London: Abacus.

Gray, B. (1989). *Collaborating: Finding Common Ground for Multiparty Problems*. San Francisco: Jossey-Bass.

Gulati, R., Puranam, P., & Tushman, M. (2012). Meta-organization design: Rethinking design in interorganizational and community contexts. *Strategic Management Journal*, 33(6), 571-586.

Heifetz, R., Grashow, A., Linsky, M. (2009). *The Practice of Adaptive leadership: Tools and Tactics for Changing Your Organization and the World*. Boston, Massachusetts: Harvard Business School Publishing.

Kegan, R., & Laskow, L. (2001). The Real Reason People Won't Change. *Harvard Business Review*, Nov 2001.

Long, S. (2013). *Socioanalytic Methods: Discovering the Hidden in Organisations and Social Systems*. London: Karnac.

Morieux, Y., & Tollman, P. (2014). *Six simple rules: How to manage complexity without getting complicated*. Boston, MA: Harvard Business Review Press.

Mortensen, M. (2012). From Teams to Recombinant Collaboration: Understanding the Evolution of Organizational Work. INSEAD *Working Papers Collection*, (2), 1-31.

Narayanan, C. (2015). Mastering Silos. *Business Today*, 24(22), 212.

Page, M. (2003). Leadership and collaboration challenges in not for profit partnerships. *Organisational and Social Dynamics*, 3(2), 207–225.

Pennec, M., & Raufflet, E. (2016). Value creation in inter-organizational collaboration: An empirical study. *Journal Of Business Ethics*.

Prins, S. (2006). The psychodynamic perspective in organizational research: Making sense of the dynamics of direction setting in emergent collaborative processes. *Journal Of Occupational & Organizational Psychology*, 79(3), 335-355.

Rice, A. K. (1969). Individual, Group and Inter-Group Processes, *Human Relations* Vol 22, No 6, p. 565.

Relational Coordination Theory. (n.d.). Retrieved August 06, 2020, from https://rcanalytic.com/rctheory/

Schein, H. (1990). Organizational Culture, *American Psychologist*, Vol.45, No.2, 109-119.

Tajfel, H., & Turner, J. C. (2004). The Social Identity Theory of Inter-group Behavior. In J. T. Jost, J. Sidanius, J. T. Jost, J. Sidanius (Eds.) *Political psychology: Key readings* (pp. 276-293). New York, NY: Psychology Press.

Tett, G. (2016). *The silo effect: The peril of expertise and the promise of breaking down barriers*. New York: Simon & Schuster Paperbacks.

Vansina, L., Vansina-Cobbaert, M.-J., Amado, G. and Schruijer, S. (2008). *Working across Organisational Boundaries: Understanding and Working with Inter-group Dynamics, in Psychodynamics for Consultants and Managers: From Understanding to Leading Meaningful Change*. Chichester, West Sussex, England: John Wiley & Sons, Ltd.

Vercaeren, G. (2017) *A study on the effectiveness of using projective drawings in an intervention to improve inter-group collaboration: a journey of discovery, abduction and transition*. Fontainbleau. INSEAD.

Willcock, D. (2013). *Collaborating for results: Silo working and relationships that work*. Surrey, England: Gower Published Limited.

CHAPTER 3
Humanizing CULTURE shifts

A HUMAN-centred approach to helping people
to act and focus in line with the strategy

'If you don't like something, change it. If you can't change it, change your attitude.'
— Maya Angelou

Why do people
in my organization
not act and focus
in accordance with our
strategic objectives?

What if people act and focus in line with the strategy, set the right priorities and execute the plans and decisions taken?

Why it matters

'Why don't people just do what we have previously discussed so many times?' This question pops up very often during the business discussions I have with leaders of organizations.

The impact of culture on organizational performance is hard to overstate. In fact, in a study conducted by Deloitte, 94% of executives viewed a distinct workplace culture as important to business success. The culture of an organization, 'the way we do things around here', is a quality that exerts a powerful influence on the success of any organization.

Healthy cultures enable organizations to adapt and unhealthy cultures lead to underperformance … or worse

Also, shortcomings in organizational culture are one of the main barriers to company success in the digital era. This is the central finding from McKinsey's survey of global executives, which highlighted three digital-culture deficiencies: functional and departmental silos, a fear of taking risks, and difficulty forming and acting on a single view of the customer.

I'm convinced that achieving ambitions and plans requires organizations to move beyond structures, processes, and systems. Addressing individual and collective behaviour including culture and mindsets as well as team and group dynamics is not optional.

A story to tell: Who needs to change first?

Barbara, managing director of the Italian division of a global corporation, asked my colleague Eric (who had been a consultant to them for many years) if he could help her with some important business challenges she was facing.

She shared her business strategy and plans in terms of growth ambitions. They talked about current and targeted market share, new markets, profitability, and digitalization. The vision and strategy seemed to be well thought out, with clear ambitions, project plans, deadlines and KPIs. It became clear that many changes would have to take place in the short- to medium-term.

Barbara's challenges and hopes

After Barbara had been in this role for about one and a half years, she expressed her two biggest concerns regarding the realization of her plans and ambitions to Eric. Firstly, she explained that her organization was not equipped and ready to deal with the multitude of changes ahead. Secondly, she stressed the need to change the culture of the Italian division, 'the way we do things here'. She explained that historically they were a very hierarchical organization, organized and led in a paternalistic, command-and-control, top-down manner, and they remained so. The previous managing director (who had held the position for the past nine years) applied a rather paternalistic and bureaucratic leadership style. Employees had a clear list of duties and responsibilities within the hierarchy, and were expected to follow the rules and procedures precisely as set out.

Creativity and collaboration were not encouraged at all

Risk-taking was not encouraged and mistakes were punished. Barbara also realized that there was a vast distance, disconnect and lack of trust between the different layers of the organization: the leadership team, middle management, and the rest of the organization. It remained the case that middle management was not empowered to make decisions and consequently escalated all topics (even minor ones) to higher management. This created bottlenecks, inefficiencies, and frustration. Seniority was the main criteria for promoting people to leadership and management roles. Departments worked in silos and there was little alignment on strategy and objectives. She finally mentioned that they did not have a culture of performance and that non-achievers were tolerated. In short, a lot of changes laid ahead.

The initiative focused on the emotional side of change

After the briefing, Erik, Anna (another colleague) and I joined forces to define how best to approach Barbara's challenge. We developed an approach based on a sequence of one-day sessions with three clear objectives. The focus was on (1) building change management capabilities within the organization (2) the definition of the desired culture and (3) transition towards this desired culture. We designed the sessions around basic concepts and practical tools to manage change (with a strong focus on the emotional side) and we defined a first set of relevant topics based on the initial briefing by Barbara.

Participants started with introspection, to better understand themselves in situations of change

The objective of the first session was to better understand themselves (self-awareness) in situations of change. After that, the idea was to evolve towards managing others more effectively during a change process. We were convinced that building this foundation of change management capabilities would be beneficial for any type of future change in the organization. Because of the current low level of trust between the different layers of the organization, we decided to start working with three groups based on their current hierarchical setup: The leadership team, middle managers, and non-managers. Each group would participate in three to four sessions over a period of six months.

Barbara and her HR team felt confident about the suggested approach; they confirmed that this was the appropriate starting point and investment for dealing with the two challenges we discussed. We started by scheduling about 80 one-day sessions with the three groups.

The first sessions focused on building change management capabilities starting from creating self-awareness in situations of change. We taught them to self-reflect and to go through the emotions that change can provoke. We introduced the basic change management concepts and related tools like the change curve model (Kübler-Ross), the emotional side of change (Bridges change model), how to deal with ambiguity and underlying patterns of emotions, thoughts, and assumptions driving engagement and behaviour (the concept of the iceberg).

People had lost hope and did not feel that the leadership team was able to change this

During the first sessions, we discovered interesting insights that helped us to fine-tune the approach moving forward. Firstly, we explored what we call 'the smell of the place', the subjective, emotional reality of the organization as perceived by its employees. We discovered, for example, that middle managers and non-managers expressed a high level of cynicism and frustration especially towards top management. This confirmed the great mental distance between middle managers and the leadership team, resulting in underlying frustration and even disrespect. Over time, people had lost hope and did not feel that the leadership team was able or willing to change this. We invested time in building psychological safety – the belief that you will not be punished when you speak up. We also realized that frustrations needed to be explored and complaints needed to be expressed (to some degree) before taking the next step.

We discovered loyalty, energy, cynics and victims

Secondly, we found that although middle managers showed willingness to change, they often played the role of the victim. Thirdly, we noticed that the leadership team and middle managers found it hard to do self-reflection and to understand that change starts with oneself. We realized that pushing towards personal actions in this state would not work; further awareness on this matter needed to be created first. Fourthly, the good news was that most participants were very engaged and showed a high willingness to share experiences. There was a lot of energy and a positive atmosphere in the room. We realized that this was a great source of energy and potential to make the desired changes happen. Many among them showed extremely high loyalty to the company and high willingness to take action to make change happen. They showed characteristics of truly loyal employees. Caring was the basis of their loyalty. They cared about the company and its customers, and about its mission. We felt they were still working for something greater than just themselves.

In the meantime, Barbara was promoted and replaced by a new managing director, Marco, who fully supported the direction taken by Barbara on this project.

We built further on the findings of our first sessions and shifted focus from managing self towards managing others during a change process. Also, we shifted towards discussions about the current (how things are done here) and desired culture (how things should be done) within the three groups.

The lack of dialogue between the different groups kept the unchecked assumptions and misunderstandings about each other alive

As consultants, we kept the agenda of the upcoming sessions very flexible, as a result of our previous observations and experience. For example, we realized that the mistrust between the different levels was based on many unchecked assumptions that led to typical 'us' versus 'them' thinking. Because of the trust we had built up as consultants during the different sessions, we started creating bridges and trust between the different groups, for example, by refuting incorrect assumptions and misunderstandings about the others, creating awareness about the perceptions others had about them (such as perceptions of middle managers about the executive committee, or perceptions of non-managers about middle managers). It also became clear that the leadership team had an important role to play in rebuilding trust and recreating hope within their organization.

The time was right to bring the three groups together

Eric, Anna and I felt that the moment was right for facilitating dialogue between the different groups. For our final workshop, we brought the leadership team, middle managers and non-managers together. This workshop was an important milestone in recreating hope, rebuilding dialogue, and increasing trust between one another, and they agreed on specific actions to transition towards the desired culture.

Throughout the sessions, and especially during the last workshop, we observed changes in the language used, which often indicates a shift in awareness. We built up the sessions in a way that facilitated triggering these shifts, 'Aha!' moments or tipping points for change. An example of what we observed was shifts in awareness in all three groups from 'the others need to change (first)' towards 'I need to change (as well) and have a role to play in this change'.

The proof of the pudding is in the eating

Defining a desired culture was not that difficult. We understood that the challenge lay in the implementation and embedding of the culture in the organization. Changing a culture is an adaptive challenge that is characterized by changes in people's priorities, beliefs, habits, and loyalties, and requires them to learn the process of problem definition and solution. This is why we recommend starting by implementing one (high-impact) behaviour and learning from it, while taking into account the specific context of the organization. 'Having the courage to give and accept honest feedback to each other' was the behaviour we selected to focus on first.

After this workshop, we continued working together with Marco in implementing the desired culture by focusing on the four structural conditions to make changes in mindset and behaviour work: role modelling, a compelling story, reinforcement mechanisms and skill building. We complemented these structural tactics by rolling out proven mental tools in the organization to fully embed the desired culture and make it stick.

After a year and a half, we made some final recommendations and officially handed the project over to Marco and his HR team. During our debrief at the end of the project we realized that our endless curiosity to understand the unique context (keep asking why), our ease to deal with uncertainty and uncomfortable situations combined with a mindset of respect, empathy and compassion were critical to guide them on this culture change.

Three HUMAN-centred tactics

In the section below, I will share three human-centred tactics that I found to be highly impactful in shifting culture and behaviours in organizations:

1. Start by installing psychological safety.
2. Build capabilities to deal with the emotional side of change, starting with introspection.
3. Discuss culture at the different levels of the organization simultaneously.

Below I elaborate on each of the three human-centred tactics in more detail.

TACTIC 1
Start by installing psychological safety

At the start of the project, we discovered that the middle managers and non-managers in particular expressed a high level of cynicism and frustration in general and directed this (a projection) towards top management. We realized that these frustrations needed to be explored and expressed as a first step. Therefore, we decided to give participants time to ventilate and express emotions that had been suppressed for many years. As consultants, we consciously assumed the (temporary) role of taking on the frustrations of the participants that were projected onto us. We invested substantial time in creating trust between us (as facilitators) and the group as well as within the groups. We installed psychological safety, the belief that you will not be punished when you speak up.

In a psychologically safe environment, you feel you can stick your neck out without fear of having it cut off

We set the example by sharing our own private and professional stories of changes we had gone through. My colleague Eric told his personal story about the emotions he was going through because his daughter had decided to leave the family home and move abroad. This allowed us to create trust between us and the group, to show vulnerability and set the tone regarding self-reflection. Also, other approaches like asking participants to select one picture (out of a range of pictures) that best represented 'how they feel' helped to build trust within the group and allowed them to reveal interesting insights and (learn to) understand and express their emotions. Only after this ventilation did we start to focus on building change management capabilities.

Below is an example of a tool that helps to build trust within a group. The script of the exercise is as follows:

Step 1: Each person selects one image (out of a range of images) that best represents how he/she feels right now.

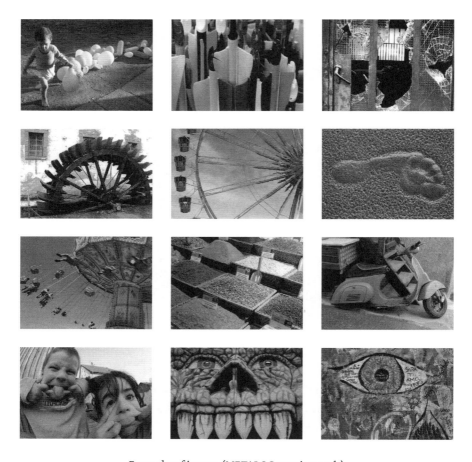

Examples of images (METALOG emotion cards)

Step 2: Split the group into pairs. Each person explains to the other person why he or she selected this image.

Step 3: Regroup and reflect (plenary) based on the following two questions:

1. What kind of insights did you get about yourself? What kind of insights did you receive about the other person?
2. How might disclosing this information about yourself improve your interactions with others?

From the second session onwards, employees opened up even more and shared their thoughts with one another. Their messages became less 'filtered'. During some of the later sessions and within some specific groups, we had to allow them (once again) the space to express frustrations as they blocked us from moving forward.

Complaining is often the result of feeling powerless

As facilitators, we had to find a balance between allowing time to blow off steam and express emotions and preventing them from lapsing into a complaining mode. We allowed ventilation of frustrations and complaints to some degree. People typically complain because they feel powerless about a specific situation. Complaining often replaces the need to act. We almost never complain directly to the person who is catalyzing the situation; we complain to people we trust – friends, family, or trusted consultants. We do not have direct conversations to solve a problem; we seek allies. We do not identify actions that could help, we blow off steam.

Asking provocative questions is a technique we applied to shift from complaining into action, or 'moving forward'. For example, we asked the group why they still wanted to work for this company when they had so many frustrations and complaints. Another technique we applied to limit complaining was to collect key messages/complaints from middle managers towards the leadership team. Afterwards we (as facilitators) would present these complaints to the leadership team – which we did.

Build capabilities to deal with the emotional side of change, starting from introspection

I have found that building a foundation of change management capabilities within organizations proves to be a good investment as it increases the success rate of any type of future change in the organization.

The first sessions focused mainly on building change management capabilities, starting from creating self-awareness in situations of change. We taught them to self-reflect and to go through the emotions that change can provoke. We introduced basic concepts and tools for managing change, which will be familiar to most readers in leadership positions. As such, I will not be discussing these here, but they are worth considering. These included the change curve model, the emotional side of change, how to deal with ambiguity and the concept of the iceberg (or how underlying patterns of emotions, thoughts, and assumptions drive engagement and behaviour). The idea was to evolve towards managing others more effectively during a change process.

> *Start by understanding your own emotions and behaviour in the context of change*

The Kübler-Ross Change Curve is a well-known model that remains relevant; we use it to create understanding of the stages of personal transition and organizational change. It helps to predict how people will react to change, so that you can help them make their own personal transitions, and make sure that they have the help and support they need.

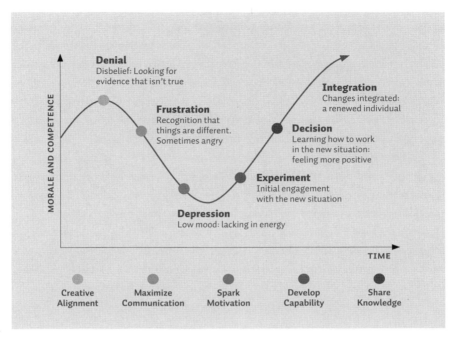

The Kübler-Ross Change Curve

Bridges' phases of transition is another well-known model we introduced and worked with during the session. Transition is the gradual, psychological reorientation process that happens as we adapt to an external change. The emotional transition process often results from a change, or occurs along with a change, but may also begin before the change takes place. Bridges argues that people in a transition go through three phases: the first phase of transition is to let go (phase 1), followed by the neutral zone, an in-between state that is full of uncertainty and confusion (phase 2). Afterwards, a new way of behaving can start (phase 3).

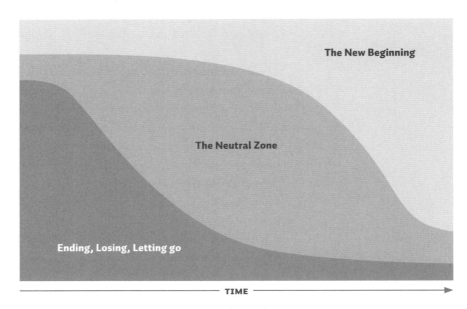

Bridges' three phases of transition

In brief, Bridges suggests that we best manage endings (phase 1) by e.g. focusing on empathy, validation and vision, to facilitate the neutral zone (phase 2) by focusing on e.g. information, communication, plans/structure, and to facilitate new beginnings (phase 3) by focusing on roles, participation and recognition.

We also worked with the metaphor of the iceberg to better understand how underlying patterns of emotions, thoughts, values and assumptions drive engagement and behaviour. These unconscious elements are often neglected but have a significant impact on the performance of organization. By doing some practical exercises, we tapped into the world of values, beliefs, emotions and hidden underlying motivational forces that influence individual and collective behaviour.

Observable behaviours
What are you doing or not doing?
How are you acting?
What are you saying?

Feelings and thoughts
What sensations and emotions are you feeling? What are you thinking or imagining? What fears do you have or what negative outcomes are you worried about?

Values and priorities
What is most important to you? In this moment? What belief do you hold about the situation, yourself and/or others?

Underlying needs
What do you really want for and from yourself? Are you aware of any deeper need, desire, intention or motivation? What experience are you wanting to create?

How mindset drives behaviour (Source: Leadership at Scale, Better Leadership, Better Results by Feser, Rennie & Nielsen)

On the next page, you will find an example of a tool that helps to create understanding of your own behaviour in the context of change. The script of the exercise is as follows:

Step 1: Have the group pair up. In pairs, talk about a personal or professional change you are currently experiencing.

Step 2: Answer the following six questions:

1. How does this change impact you? (rational perspective)
2. How do you feel about the change? (emotional perspective)
3. Where do you position yourself on the Kübler-Ross Change curve ?
4. What are you most excited about? (drivers of motivation)
5. What are you most worried about? (for example: losing autonomy or freedom, isolation or not belonging or not being valued)
6. What can you do to go to the next phase in the change curve?

Step 3: Regroup and debrief.

- What did you discover about yourself ? What did you learn?
- What are you going to do next?

Putting yourself in the shoes of the other

After having gone through the introspection phase, we shifted focus to the impact of change for the other and learning to put yourself in their shoes. Below, you will find an example of another tool that helps you to put yourself in the shoes of another (empathy). The script of this mindfulness exercise is as follows:

Step 1: Ask the group to close their eyes and read the script below very slowly:

'This is an exercise in full silence.

Please close your eyes.

Make yourself comfortable.

Recall your most recent interaction with someone in your organization.

Look around you: look in front of you, look behind you, look to your left, look to your right.

Switch places with the other person. You are now the other person.

Look around you: look in front of you, look behind you,
look to your left, look to your right.

Being this other person: What do you see? What do you think?
What do you hear? What do you feel?

Please open your eyes.'

Step 2: Write down on a post-it:

- One thought you had as the other person (post-it 1). One feeling you had as the other person (post-it 2).
- Ask the team to put all their post-its on a flipchart. Just look at it. Read what is on the flipchart. You don't need to discuss it at this stage.

Step 3: Ask the team what they learned from doing this exercise and what they are going to do next.

TACTIC 3
Discuss culture at the different levels of the organization simultaneously

DEFINING YOUR DESIRED CULTURE IS NOT THAT DIFFICULT

The culture of an organization significantly influences its decisions and actions. An organization's prevailing ideas, values, attitudes, and beliefs guide the way its employees think, feel, and act – quite often unconsciously. Culture is considered the 'glue' that holds an organization together and for others, the 'compass' that provides direction.

'How we do things around here'

Edgar Schein defines culture as a pattern of shared basic assumptions that the group learned as it solved its problems of external adaptation and internal integration, that has worked well enough to be considered valid and, therefore, to be taught to new members as the correct way to perceive, think, and feel in relation to those problems. There are three distinct levels in organizational cultures as shown in the figure below.

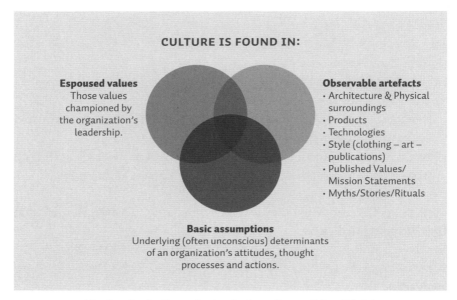

The three levels of organizational culture (Source: Edgar Schein)

PAUSE FOR INSIGHTS
A famous 'Social Experiment'

The famous 'Social Experiment' of the five monkeys and a ladder explains how culture works. A group of scientists placed five monkeys in a cage, and in the middle, a ladder with bananas on top. Every time a monkey went up the ladder, the scientists soaked the rest of the monkeys with cold water. After a while, every time a monkey would start up the ladder, the others would pull it down and beat it up. After a time, no monkey would dare to try climbing the ladder, no matter how great the temptation. The scientists then decided to replace one of the monkeys. The first thing this new monkey did was start to climb the ladder. Immediately, the others pulled him down and beat him up. After several beatings, the new monkey learned never to go up the ladder, even though there was no evident reason not to, aside from the beatings. The second monkey was substituted and the same occurred. The first monkey participated in the beating of the second monkey. A third monkey was changed and the same was repeated. The fourth monkey was changed, resulting in the same, before the fifth was finally replaced as well. What was left was a group of five monkeys that – without ever having received a cold shower – continued to beat up any monkey who attempted to climb the ladder. If it was possible to ask the monkeys why they beat up all those who attempted to climb the ladder, their most likely answer would be 'I don't know. It's just how things are done around here.'

The most damaging phrase in the language is: 'It's always been done that way'

How does culture impact organizational performance? Carolyn Taylor clearly explains what behaviour is and its role in the performance of an organization. In summary, she argues that behaviour is how we act. She analyzed many lists of behaviours used in organizations and grouped these into three categories:

1. Interactions with others.
2. Use of time.
3. Making decisions.

As shown in the figure on the next page, these behaviours impact personal contribution and the results of an organization. Mindset is the driver of behaviours. This brings us to the most challenging and important part of a culture implementation plan. What people do is caused by who they are. This third level of the model shown in the figure is called BE. How someone is at the BE-level determines what they DO which determines the outcomes they HAVE. The BE-level – being the mindset – contains three elements: feelings, values and beliefs, and the level of consciousness.

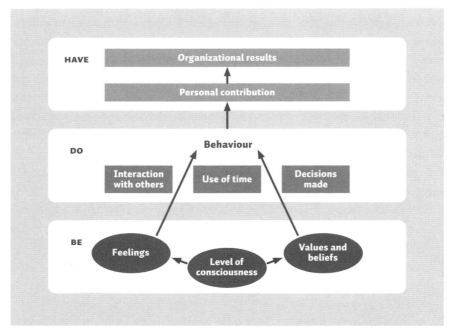

The BE-DO-HAVE model (Source: Walking the talk, building a culture for success by Carolyn Taylor)

We defined the following six desired behaviours for Marco's organization as follows:

- Passion for customers, excellence in the pursuit of their satisfaction.
- Passion and empathy in every one-to-one interaction, with respect for the other person.
- No fear in behaviour and interaction. No fear to speak to my manager or the manager of my manager.
- Integrity in relations with other departments.
- Courage to give and accept honest feedback.
- Courage to speak up and give your personal opinion.

During the culture definition work sessions, we applied the following script for each of these desired behaviours to make them more explicit and make sure these are understood in the same way.

Step 1: Select a desired behaviour you want to elaborate on.

Step 2: Answer the questions: What do you want to SEE? And, what don't you want to SEE?

Step 3: Answer the questions: What do you want people to SAY? And, what don't you want people to SAY?

Step 4: Answer the questions: What do you want people to THINK? And, what don't you want people to THINK?

I experienced that answering these questions deepens the understanding of what is meant by the desired behaviour. I learned that reflection on what you do not want to see, hear or have people think is often easier than reflecting on what you want to see, hear or have people in your organization think.

PAUSE FOR INSPIRATION
The 'attitude' challenge of your hiring process – and three things you can do about it

A promising new hire with a proven track record who ends up as a failure at your company – does this sound familiar? In my daily consulting work, I often see this painful problem. A survey that Wouter van Essenberg and I conducted on this business-critical topic shows that 45% of executives are confronted with hiring misfits.

THE HIGH COST OF A BAD HIRE

Hiring the wrong person is one of the most time-consuming and costly mistakes you can make. Apart from the direct financial hit, significant hidden costs will permeate the organization due to the loss of time and energy, disrupted client relationships, reduced productivity and morale, and culture degradation. Moreover, these negative effects are amplified in the case of roles at senior leadership level because of the increased influence they have. 'The financial losses resulting from hiring a misfit are tremendous, not to mention the operational and emotional disruption caused to the organization and its people.'

IT IS ALL ABOUT ATTITUDE!

Attitude is *the* differentiating factor for performance at work, both positive and negative.

75% of our respondents identify attitude as the factor that created the greatest degree of differentiation in the performance of their best employees *(Exhibit 1)*. Having a continuous learning mindset was mentioned most frequently, followed by having a positive attitude, being a team player and being results oriented.

Additionally, in terms of disqualifying characteristics, the number one reason for hiring misfits is a mismatch in attitude, mindset, and/or cultural fit, mentioned by 84% of executives *(Exhibit 2)*. In addition, a lack of communication skills is also frequently mentioned as an important cause for hiring misfits.

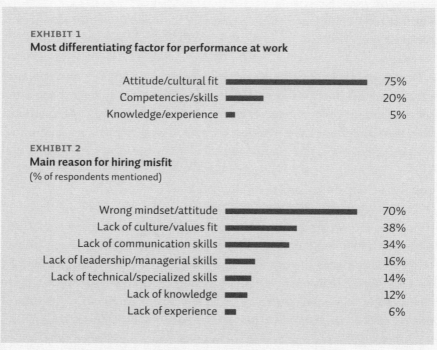

Exhibit 1: The differentiating factor for performance at work
Exhibit 2: Main reasons for hiring misfits

THE HIRING CHALLENGE IS ALL ABOUT ATTITUDE … AGAIN!

Respondents say that mindset/attitude fit (52%) and culture/value fit (46%) are the qualities that are most difficult to evaluate (*Exhibit 3*).

When there is strong pressure to hire, the problem gets even worse: 36% of respondents start to compromise on mindset/attitude or culture/value fit.

Finally, 67% of respondents recognize that they sometimes feel something is not right and find difficulty in naming it after an interview.

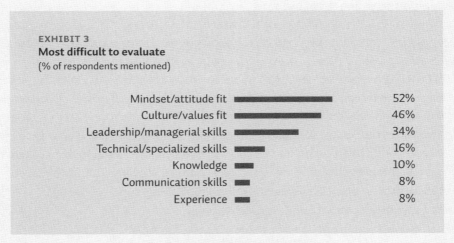

EXHIBIT 3
Most difficult to evaluate
(% of respondents mentioned)

Mindset/attitude fit	52%
Culture/values fit	46%
Leadership/managerial skills	34%
Technical/specialized skills	16%
Knowledge	10%
Communication skills	8%
Experience	8%

Exhibit 3: Most difficult to evaluate

HOW TO AVOID PENGUINS IN THE DESERT

Three things you can do to avoid attitude misfits:

1. GO BEYOND THE STANDARD JOB DESCRIPTION

Create a baseline that explicitly specifies the differentiating factors for success in terms of attitude, values and motivational context in each job profile.

Since this is not common practice, companies may find it difficult to do this. In fact, creating such a baseline is very doable, using techniques such as conducting cultural values assessments and interviewing key stakeholders within the company.

Once the baseline has been created, it can be translated into wanted and unwanted behaviours one can evaluate using quantitative and qualitative methods that tap into the world of values, beliefs, emotions and hidden underlying motivational forces of the candidate. Examples of these techniques are the standard (STAR) interviewing method, personal values assessment or insight generating discussions on attitude fit using drawings (for example, self-portraits) or a set of pictures.

2. BUILD 'ATTITUDE ASSESSMENT' COMPETENCY IN YOUR ORGANIZATION

Increase the awareness level within your company about critical success factors for performance and/or misfit and make sure that the baseline and associated wanted and unwanted behaviours are thoroughly understood by everyone involved in the hiring process. In addition, get every person involved in hiring interviews up to standard on interviewing skills and personal (unconscious) biases. Interviewing and evaluating behaviours is a skill, but it is a skill you can learn.

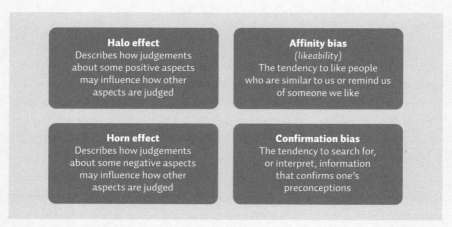

Four important biases during a hiring process (Source: A Head for Hiring: The Behavioural Science of Recruitment and Selection by Linos & Reinhard)

3. A STRUCTURED HIRING PROCESS PAYS OFF

Having a structured and standardized approach for conducting hiring interviews and getting to hiring decisions as well as holding structured training and evaluation programmes for interviewers are mandatory if you want to professionalize your hiring process. Think of it. We do this for virtually all other business processes, be it sales, production, or IT development. Your hiring process deserves to be taken seriously too.

THE PROOF OF THE PUDDING IS IN THE EATING

Below, I will share some lessons we learned in making culture change stick. First, we discovered the power of working with values in a culture change journey. Secondly, we suggest applying four structural conditions to make changes in mindset and behaviour work: role modelling, fostering understanding and conviction, reinforcement with formal mechanisms and development of talent and skills. Thirdly, do not underestimate the impact of middle management. Finally, we recommend to apply nudging techniques and the roll-out of mental tools (two in particular) within the organization to ensure your desired culture gets fully embedded.

The power of working with values

I like to share a case with you that shows how we used values to define and transition to the desired culture in a project. Understanding the personal, perceived and desired values of an organization gives important insights about the 'glue' connecting team members at a deeper level, how the organization is experienced today, potential sources of frustration (so called 'hot buttons') and how the organization can reach its highest effectiveness.

Personal values reflect what is important to us. They are a shorthand way of describing our individual motivations. Together with our beliefs, they are an important factor that drives how we act and behave. Common personal values are the 'glue' connecting employees in an organization at a deeper level.

Below, you will find an example of a common personal values assessment of an organization. **Employees were asked:** Which of the following values and behaviours most represent who you are?

Personal values	Percentage	Ranking
Taking responsibility	52%	1
Humour/Fun	37%	2
Continuous learning	35%	3
Enthusiasm	34%	4
Respect	34%	4
Efficiency	33%	5

Assessment of personal values (top 5 ranking) (Source: Barrett Values Centre)

If employees act in a manner that goes against an important common value (such as taking responsibility), they will most probably react very emotionally, which might trigger (often unconsciously) ineffective behaviours.

Current values indicate how the organization is perceived and experienced today.

An example of the perceived current values assessment follows below. **The question put to employees was:** Which of the following values and behaviours most represent how the organization works today?

Current values	Percentage	Ranking
Creativity	61%	1
Ambition	54%	2
Entrepreneurship	50%	3
Being the best	43%	4
Quality	40%	5

Assessment of perceived current values of the organization (top 5 ranking)
(Source: Barrett Values Centre)

In this example, creativity is the most important current value followed by ambition, entrepreneurship, being the best, and quality.

Desired values indicate what are perceived as essential values in order to achieve the organization's highest objectives. **Employees were asked:** Which of the following values and behaviours are essential for the organization to achieve its highest performance?

Desired values	Percentage	Ranking
Creativity	56%	1
Coaching/Mentoring	48%	2
Collaboration/Respect/Vision	40%	3
Efficiency	39%	4
Balance (Work/Life)	37%	5

Assessment of desired values of the organization (top 5 ranking)
Source: Barrett Values Centre)

In this example, creativity is the most important desired value followed by coaching/mentoring, collaboration, respect, vision, efficiency and work/life balance.

Value jumps. The difference between desired and current values indicates several relevant jumps for the organization. Coaching/mentoring is the value with the highest difference between desired and current value. Employees also see greater efficiency, balance (home/work), open communication and cooperation as essential to achieve the organization's objectives. The percentage of personal value gives an indication of the complexity/ease of entering this value and related behaviour. The higher the percentage, the easier it must be to include this in the organization. Increasing efficiency would therefore be relatively easy.

Values	Current	Desired	Delta	Personal
Coaching/mentoring	4%	48%	-44%	9%
Efficiency	9%	39%	-30%	33%
Balance (work/life)	9%	37%	-28%	13%
Open communication	6%	33%	-27%	21%
Collaboration	17%	40%	-23%	27%

'Value jumps' (Source: Barrett Values Centre)

Hot buttons. The difference between personal and current values indicates the 'hot buttons', which are possible sources of frustration for employees.

Values	Current	Desired	Delta
Taking responsibility	13%	52%	-39%
Continuous learning	5%	35%	-30%
Honesty	4%	29%	-26%
Efficiency	9%	33%	-24%
Adaptability	1%	20%	-18%

'Hot buttons' (Source: Barrett Values Centre)

Employees indicate that they want to take more responsibility, learn more 'continuously', want to see more honesty, efficiency, and adaptability within the organization. The fact that this is only available to a limited extent gives rise to possible frustrations.

Four structural conditions to change mindsets and behaviours

Mckinsey's influence model says that four key actions influence employee mindsets and behaviour. I find it a very powerful model, and I often use it in initiatives to change mindset and behaviour. They state that employees will alter their mindsets only if they see the point of the change and agree with it – at least enough to give it a try. The surrounding structures (reward and recognition systems, for example) must be in tune with the new behaviour, and employees must have the appropriate skills. The final requirement they give is that employees must see people they respect actively modelling the changes. In the outline of the model, it is also noted that each of these conditions is realized independently, but together they add up to a way of changing the behaviour of people in organizations by changing attitudes about what can and should happen at work.

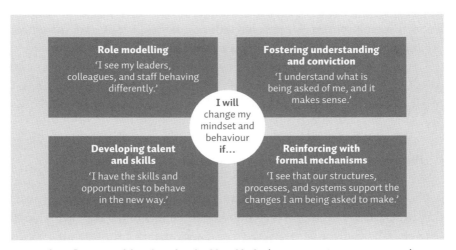

The influence model with its four building blocks (Source: McKinsey & Company)

(1) Role modelling

In any organization, people model their behaviour on 'significant others': those they see in positions of influence. Within a single organization, people in different functions or levels choose different role models. So, to change behaviour consistently throughout an organization, it is not enough to ensure that people at the top are in line with the new ways of working; role models at every level must 'walk the talk'.

The way role models deal with their tasks can vary, but the underlying values informing their behaviour must be consistent. Behaviour in organizations is deeply affected not only by role models but also by the groups with which people identify. Role modelling by individuals must therefore be confirmed by the groups that surround them if it is to have a permanent or deep influence. Change must be meaningful to key groups at each level of the organization. A common misunderstanding is that role modelling refers only to role modelling by leaders. It can be done by anyone in the organization. Nevertheless, we know that the impact of the behaviour of leaders on others is significant. As I will elaborate on in chapter 4, every day, throughout organizations, leaders make many decisions; these decisions involve interactions; and each of these can either support or harm the main effort of the organization. Because of the role modelling dimension of leadership, the impact of the behaviour of one single leader on the whole organization can be huge in a positive or negative sense.

Also, Carolyn Taylor explains in a truly clear way how the change in mindset of a leader leads to new performance outcomes (see figure opposite).

(2) Fostering understanding and conviction

Keller argues that if people in an organization believe in its overall purpose, they will be happy to change their individual behaviour to serve that purpose – indeed, they will suffer from cognitive dissonance if they do not. But to feel comfortable about change and to carry it out with enthusiasm, people must understand the role of their actions in the unfolding drama of the company's fortunes and believe that it is worthwhile for them to play a part.

> Change in the mindset of leaders
> **Leads to**
> Change in the behaviour of these leaders
> **Leads to**
> Different decisions being made by these leaders, in line with
> their new beliefs and values
> **Leads to**
> People attributing meaning to these decisions (symbols)
> associated with a change in values
> **Leads to**
> New messages being received throughout the organization
> about what is now valued (supported by changing enablers
> which have simultaneously been redesigned)
> **Leads to**
> Other people in the organization changing their behaviour
> to fit into the new norms
> **Leads to**
> Further reinforcement that the culture and its values have now changed
> **Leads to**
> New performance outcomes, the effect of the chosen values

The domino effect (Source: Walking the talk, building a culture for success by Carolyn Taylor)

It is not enough to tell employees that they will have to do things differently. Anyone leading a major change programme must take the time to think through the organization's 'story' – what makes it worth undertaking – and to explain that story to all those involved in making change happen, so that their contributions make sense to them as individuals.

(3) Reinforcement with formal mechanisms

Organizational designers agree that reporting structures, management and operational processes, and measurement procedures – setting targets, measuring performance, and granting financial and non-financial rewards – must be consistent with the behaviour that people are asked to embrace. When a company's goals for new behaviour are not reinforced, employees are less likely to adopt it consistently; if managers are urged to spend more time coaching junior staff, for instance, but coaching doesn't figure in the performance scorecards of managers, they are not likely to bother.

(4) Developing talent and skills

How can adults best be equipped with the skills they need to make relevant changes in behaviour? First, give them time. Kolb showed that adults can't learn merely by listening to instructions; they must also absorb the new information, use it experimentally, and integrate it with their existing knowledge. In practice, this means that you cannot teach everything there is to know about a subject in one session. Much better to break down the formal teaching into chunks, with time in between for the learners to reflect, experiment, and apply the new principles. Large-scale change happens only in steps.

The impact of middle management

I experience that middle managers are often in difficult, frustrating situations. They are often squeezed, 'stuck in the middle', between top management and the rest of the organization. Although there are many discussions going on about the role and value of middle managers, we find that they are in a challenging role and can play an important part in implementing (culture) change programmes.

In his research at INSEAD, Professor Quy Nguyen Huy argues that managers are often cast as dinosaurs, 'has-beens'. Mediocre managers and intermediaries who defend the status quo instead of supporting others' attempts to change organizations for the better. He has examined this interesting breed of manager – in particular, middle managers' roles during periods of radical organizational change. His findings will surprise many. Middle managers, it turns out, make valuable contributions to the realization of radical change at companies – contributions that go largely unrecognized by most senior executives.

Quy Nguyen Huy says these contributions occur in four major areas. First, middle managers often have good entrepreneurial ideas that they are able and willing to realize – if only they can get a hearing. Second, they're far better than most senior executives at leveraging the informal networks at companies that make substantive, lasting change. Because they have worked their way up the corporate ladder, middle managers' networks run deep. Third, they stay attuned to employees' emotional needs during organizational change, thereby maintaining the transformation's momentum. And finally, they manage the tension between continuity and change – they keep the organization from falling into extreme inertia or extreme chaos.

Applying nudging techniques to change behaviour

Nudging is a concept in behavioural economics, political theory, and behavioural sciences that proposes positive reinforcement and indirect suggestions as ways to influence the behaviour and decision making of groups or individuals. It is a non–intrusive mental push that helps the brain make better decisions, and is intended to help people change behaviour, without convincing them with rational arguments, incentives, or threatening or punishing them.

The nudge concept was popularized by Thaler and Sunstein in their book: *Nudge: Improving Decisions About Health, Wealth, and Happiness*. Richard Thaler, winner of the Nobel Prize in behavioural economics in 2018, and other behavioural economists argue that people make decisions quickly under pressure, based largely on intuition, and are unconsciously guided by biases and psychological fallacies. Organizations can use this concept to grasp the relationship between mindset and behavioural change and can employ it to address unconscious bias and instincts. Some people worry and see it as a paternalistic, manipulative practice. From an ethical perspective, you might want to have a discussion on how to deal with it responsibly before you start using this technique.

Strategically designed nudges can effectively influence behaviour and drive results in solving pressing issues of organizations

Using 'nudges' can be the key to opening up creativity, innovation and increased performance at an individual, team, inter-team (collaboration) or organizational level. It can support dealing with organizational challenges with regard to motivation, diversity and inclusion, well-being or shifting towards the critical desired behaviours supporting your strategy. In the story I told above, Marco's organization had to make the shift towards a mindset and behaviour focusing on passion for customers, empathy in one-on-one action, speaking up, having the courage to give and accept feedback, etc.

To demonstrate how subtle nudges can have remarkable results, a leading consulting firm put the concept of 'nudging' to the test during a gathering of senior executives at one of their leadership programmes. They prepared a nudging experiment for this group before they introduced participants to the ideas around the predictable irrationality of humans and the unconscious biases we carry, as well as the nudging method. They split the executives into two groups, and each group was asked to work in pairs to develop ideas for the Executive Leadership Programme for ten minutes. They considered the groups equally talented and motivated with similar intrinsic enthusiasm. But each received different approaches to their instructions, and they also changed their environment.

: *Boost a team's creative thinking by passing around warm mugs of tea*

The first group received a warm, welcoming appeal, with a blue note saying 'Hello!', 'We need your help' and 'Thank you'. They were handed warm tea or coffee and were encouraged to offer drinks to others. These executives were asked to put individual ideas on post-it notes using coloured pencils. Members of the second group received bureaucratic instructions, emphasizing that they should 'Please adhere to these instructions during the session on ideation' and 'Ensure you are properly hydrated during the session.' These executives were told to to write 'clearly listed and numbered' ideas on the white-lined paper they were given. They were served ice water.

: *Small changes in stimuli can lead to notable differences in outcomes*

The results were clear: The positively primed first group developed 70 completely new ideas that covered new territories, more than twice the 32 fresh ideas of the second group, whose members focused mainly on structural or logistical improvements. They learned that even the most seasoned business professionals can benefit from the positive effects of nudging and that small changes in stimuli/environment can lead to appreciable differences in outcomes.

Rolling out mental tools throughout the organization

As explained before, it is critical to identify the type of challenges to change you are facing: adaptive or technical. A technical challenge is defined as those that can be solved by the knowledge of experts, whereas the adaptive challenge requires learning during the process of problem definition and solution. Realizing culture shifts should be seen as an adaptive challenge that requires learning the process of problem definition and solution.

Along with the adaptive challenge goes the adaptive leadership style. In terms of leadership development, Marco had to learn to practise an adaptive leadership style and develop the ability to deal effectively with ambiguity, uncertainty and tensions, which were unavoidable realities of the culture change journey.

I have positive experiences with rolling out three impactful mental tools that create awareness and learning about one's own and others' behavioural dynamics. They facilitate the process to fully embed them in the way of operating.

MENTAL TOOL 1
Fact check your assumptions and beliefs

This mental tool allows you to modify and change feelings by means of logical deductive reasoning, instead of allowing your feelings to get the better of you. It allows you to tune in to the inner dialogue, the belief system that is responsible for your feelings and behaviour. At an individual level, Howard Book describes a fundamental framework, known as ABCDE, a system for altering perceptions, attitudes, and behaviours, pioneered by Dr Albert Ellis.

In the ABCDE Model, this is what a typical series of thoughts might look like:

- **A:** Activating Event: something happens to or around someone.
- **B:** Belief: the event causes someone to have a belief, either rational or irrational.
- **C:** Consequence: the belief has led to a consequence, with rational beliefs leading to healthy consequences and irrational beliefs leading to unhealthy consequences.
- **D:** Disputation: if one has held an irrational belief that has caused unhealthy consequences, they must dispute that belief and turn it into a rational belief.
- **E:** New Effect: the disputation has turned the irrational belief into a rational belief, and the person now has healthier consequences of their belief as a result.

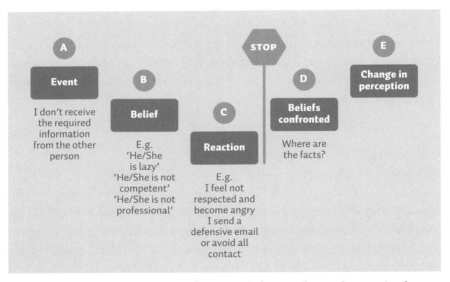

The ABCDE model by Dr Albert Ellis – Example (Source: The EQ Edge: Emotional Intelligence and Your Success by Book, Stein & Steven)

In brief, our behaviour is often driven by assumptions that are often not checked against reality. Being conscious of your assumptions might help to avoid ineffective behaviours.

The principle of charity

What do you see in the picture below?

(Source: Jospeh Jastrow)

Some people see a duck, some others see a rabbit. It shows that our observation is selective and distorted. Also, communication is ambiguous. When you listen to someone, you hear what you hear through your own filters. And, you know that when the other responds to you, he/she applies his/her own filters.

'We don't see things as they are, we see them as we are' – Anais Nin

Our unconscious mind acts as a filter to select the information that can enter our conscious mind by using defence mechanisms like deletion, generalization, distortion, intellectualization, projection, etc. The result is the internal representation, or our conscious experience. Typical examples you might recognize are: You just bought a new car, suddenly you see the same type of car everywhere or we tend to remember our past experiences rosier than it actually was. Most of the time, you do not consciously think about these processes, you just 'act'.

The mental tool 'Principle of charity' is somewhat related to the previous mental tool and offers a simple methodological prescription for fighting our natural tendency to treat our own interpretations as facts. It relies on the acknowledgement that our mind is a translator and one that is prone to making mistakes. INSEAD's professor Neil Bearden calls this idea 'the principle of charity': you should try to interpret the statements and actions of people in a way that maximizes the reasonableness of those statements and actions.

The principle of charity is about actively finding an interpretation that makes the person reasonable.

It is about being aware that in almost every interaction there are unchecked assumptions, duck-rabbit misunderstandings, ambiguity, and filtered observations. It is about developing the capacity to actively deal with this. The underlying assumption is based on two principles: (1) most of the time, what people say is true and (2) most people are good people (with good intentions). I experienced in many interventions with clients that exercising 'the principle of charity' mitigates potential misunderstandings and significantly impacts the effectiveness of interactions between people. Try it out!

Find your hidden competing commitment

This mental tool is an introspective exercise to better understand the hidden competing commitments that make it hard to change your behaviour. It is about creating awareness about what (unconsciously) blocks you to make the change (immunity to change).

In the book *The Real Reason People Won't Change*, Kegan and Lahey show how our individual beliefs, along with the collective mindsets in organizations combine to create a natural but powerful immunity to change. They assert that change is extremely difficult, be it on the personal or the organizational level, due to hidden competing commitments, sweeping assumptions and ingrained thought patterns that discourage individuals and teams from abandoning the status quo.

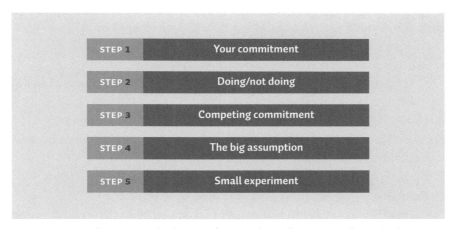

Immunity to change map: the five steps (Source: The Real Reason People Won't Change by Kegan & Laskow)

Below, you will find an example of a tool that helps to find competing commitments. The script to follow is this:

Step 1 – Your commitment: Select a behaviour you want to change for yourself.

Examples:
- I want to be more available and visible to the team.
- I really want to be available to the team because this is the kind of leader I want to be.

Step 2 – Doing/Not doing: What are you doing or not doing that prevents you from applying this behaviour?

Examples:
- I avoid the coffee machine, I'm too busy with my tasks, and I work in my closed office.
- I don't walk around or engage in small talk; I avoid informal meetings.

Step 3 – Competing commitment: What might be a worry, discomfort, something you fear if you would apply your desired behaviour?

Example:
- I'm perceived as distant and uninterested. People don't know what I'm doing.

Step 4 – The big assumption: What is the worst thing that could happen if you applied your desired behaviour?

Examples:
- I may be put in a position where I'm asked questions that I can't answer. Others might question me as a leader.
- If I'm at the coffee machine, people will think I'm not working hard.

Step 5 – Small experiment: What small steps can you take towards applying the new behaviour?

Examples:
- Have lunch with someone from my team.
- Take the initiative to invite a member of my team for coffee.

Changes in the language as indicators of critical shifts

Back to the story. We built up the sessions in such a way as to create these shifts in awareness. These shifts then led to 'Aha!' moments, tipping points for change.

Two examples of shifts in awareness we created during the sessions were:

- Shifts from 'the others (and especially upper management) need to change (first)' towards 'I need to change (as well) and have a role to play in this change'.
- Shifts from 'if the situation is clear and stable, I will change' towards 'I need to change and can make a difference in the current context'.

During discussions, it is important to listen very carefully to changes in wording. Language is an important indicator of shifts in awareness. I would like to share an anecdote from one of the sessions, which describes it clearly. It is a memorable moment where one of the middle managers shared that he took over a project that was initiated by one of his employees. He assumed that the employee did not have the skills to manage the implementation. The project was important, so the manager moved ahead and successfully implemented the project himself, without involvement of the employee. The relationship with that employee was very difficult afterwards, and they were not able to work together for an entire year. The manager understood that he had made a mistake by assuming that the employee was not able or willing to take responsibility for the project. The manager shared that he should have talked to the employee sooner, to prevent this misunderstanding. When this manager made himself vulnerable by admitting that he had made a mistake in his people management role, this was a great turning point during the workshop.

This example and the language he used showed two things. First of all, it showed that he felt safe to share a personal failure (psychological safety). Secondly, he became aware that he had an important role to play to make the change happen. He did not find an excuse in the context, and did not expect others to change (first).

← PREVIOUS PAGES

Peter's narrative

Introspection and Self-awareness

In a period of change, managers broaden
their behaviours through the activity of
drawing (effective in real time or online) to
encourage self-awareness and introspection.
As a result, they engage more deeply with
each other's creativity, strengthening
empathy within the team.

Summarizing the main points

- **'The way we do things around here'**, the culture of an organization is a quality that exerts a powerful influence on the success of any organization.

- **'Why don't people just do what we have previously discussed so many times?'** This question pops up very often during discussions I have with leaders of organizations.

- **Three HUMAN-centred tactics** that I found to be highly impactful in changing the culture of an organization are:

  1. Start by installing psychological safety.
  2. Build capabilities to deal with the emotional side of change, starting with introspection.
  3. Discuss culture at the different levels of the organization simultaneously.

- **Defining your desired culture is the easy part. The proof of the pudding is in the eating.** Embedding new behaviours is a challenging journey, but achievable.

- **A flexible approach to implementing shifts in culture pays off.** Start by exploring the organizational context, installing psychological safety and building awareness and capabilities about the emotional side of change. I learned that keeping an open mind throughout the whole journey and refining the approach based on the insights discovered is essential for success.

- I recommend **working with values** as they are a great source of insights on the shift in critical behaviours that need to be made.

- **The four structural conditions to change mindset and behaviour are:** (1) Role modelling (2) fostering understanding and conviction (3) reinforcement through formal mechanisms and (4) development of talent and skills.

- **Conscious involvement of middle management, applying nudging techniques and rolling out mental tools** throughout the organization are worth considering in order to make shifts in behaviours stick.

- **Look out for changes in language.** They are good indicators of shifts in awareness, which lead to tipping points for change. An important shift in awareness to be made in this kind of transition is from 'the others need to change' towards 'I need to change'.

►How to get started

TACTIC 1
Start by installing psychological safety

► **Evaluate the psychological safety in your organization.**

How would you score the statements below on a scale from 1 (Strongly Disagree) to 5 (Strongly Agree)? Use the statements below as a reference for reflection.

1. When someone makes a mistake in my organization, it is never held against him or her. SCORE:_____
2. In my organization, it is easy to discuss difficult issues and problems. SCORE:_____
3. In my organization, people are rarely rejected for being different. SCORE:_____
4. It is completely safe to take a risk in my organization. SCORE:_____
5. It is easy to ask other members of my organization for help. SCORE:_____
6. Members of my organization value and respect each other's contributions. SCORE:_____

(Source: Amy C. Edmondson, The Fearless Organization Scan)

What did you discover? What do you suggest undertaking to increase the psychological safety in your organization?

TACTIC 2
Build capabilities to deal with the emotional side of change, starting with introspection

▶ **Some introspection: Think about a professional or private change/ transition you are currently experiencing.**

Please answer the following six questions:

1. How does this change impact you?
2. How do you feel about the change?
3. Where are you positioned on the Kübler-Ross Change curve? (Shock, Denial, Frustration, Depression, Experiment, Decision, or Integration)
4. What are you most excited about?
5. What are you most worried about?
6. What can you do to go to the next phase in the change curve?

What did you discover about yourself in situations of change, the way you experience this change and what could help you to deal with changes even more effectively?

TACTIC 3
Discuss culture at the different levels of the organization simultaneously

▶ **Find out 'The way things are done around here'.** Which of the following values and behaviours most represent how your organization works today? Please select maximum 10 values.

- accountability
- achievement
- adaptability
- balance (home/work)
- being the best
- blame
- brand image
- bureaucracy
- caring
- caution
- clarity
- coaching/mentoring
- commitment
- community involvement
- compassion
- conflict resolution
- confusion
- continuous improvement
- continuous learning
- control
- cooperation
- cost reduction
- courage
- creativity
- cross group collaboration
- curiosity
- customer collaboration
- customer satisfaction
- ease with uncertainty
- efficiency
- embracing diversity
- empire building
- employee engagement
- employee fulfilment
- employee health
- employee recognition
- empowerment
- encouragement
- enthusiasm
- entrepreneurial
- environmental awareness
- equality
- ethics
- excellence
- experience
- exploitation
- fairness
- financial stability
- forgiveness
- future generations
- global leadership
- goals orientation
- hierarchy
- holistic thinking
- honesty
- human rights
- humour/fun
- inclusiveness
- information hoarding
- information sharing
- initiative
- innovation
- integrity
- internal competition
- job insecurity
- leadership development
- leading by example
- listening
- long hours
- long-term perspective
- making a difference
- manipulation
- mission focus
- open communication
- openness
- organizational growth
- patience
- personal growth
- positive attitude
- power
- productivity
- professional growth
- professionalism
- profit
- quality
- respect
- results orientation
- risk taking
- safety
- shared values
- shared vision
- short-term focus
- silo mentality
- social responsibility
- strategic alliances
- sustainability
- teamwork
- transparency
- trust
- well-being (physical/emotional/mental/spiritual)
- wisdom

(Source: Barrett Values Centre)

▶ **Brainstorm about the desired behaviours in your organization; the ones that ensure that organizational ambitions will be achieved.**

Tip: You can start by using the list of values on the previous page or think about specific behaviours related to (1) interactions with others (2) use of time (3) decision making.

▶ **Please select the one change in behaviour that will have the biggest positive impact on the performance of your organization.**

For this selected behaviour, please answer the three questions below:

· What do you want to SEE? And, what don't you want to SEE ?
· What do you want people to SAY? And, what don't you want people to SAY ?
· What do you want people to THINK? And, what don't you want people to THINK?

▶ **Take a step back and define the key insights you discovered about changing your culture?** Please describe.

▶ **Building your change plan:** Refine your approach to make the change in behaviour happen and include structural and behavioural tactics to make this change in behaviour.

Tip: Think about structural tactics related to leadership role modelling, building a compelling story, reinforcement mechanisms and skills building.

▶ **What did you learn? What are you going to do next?**

....
....
....
....
....

Good luck!

'Do not tolerate brilliant jerks.
The cost to teamwork is too high.'

– Reed Hastings, CEO, Netflix

Chapter 3: **Key references and interesting reads**

Amado, G., & Ambrose, A. (Eds.). (2001). *The transitional approach to change.* London: Karnac.

Basford, T., & Schaninger, B. (2016, April 11). The four building blocks of change. Retrieved December 13, 2020, from https://www.mckinsey.com/business-functions/organization/our-insights/the-four-building-blocks--of-change

Berinato, S. (2020). That Discomfort You're Feeling Is Grief. Retrieved from https://hbr.org/2020/03/that-discomfort-youre-feeling-is-grief

Bridges, W., & Mitchel, S. (2000), Leading Transition : A New Model for Change. *Leader to Leader*, Nr. 16.

Collins, J. C., & Porras, J. I. (1997). *Built to last: Successful habits of visionary companies.* New York: Harper Business.

Dillon, R., Sperling, J., & Tietz, J. (2018). A small nudge to create stunning team results. Mckinsey Organization blog.

Feser, C., Rennie, M., & Nielsen, N. C. (2019). *Leadership at Scale Better leadership, better results.* Place of publication not identified: Hachee Books Ireland.

Galef, B. G. (1976). Social Transmission of Acquired Behavior: A Discussion of Tradition and Social Learning in Vertebrates. *Advances in the Study of Behavior*, 77-100. doi:10.1016/s0065-3454(08)60082-0

Gladwell, M. (2015). *The tipping point: How little things can make a big difference.* London: Abacus.

Goran, J., LaBerge, L., & Srinivasan, R. (2017, July 20). Culture for a digital age. Retrieved December 13, 2020, from https://www.mckinsey.com/business-functions/mckinsey-digital/our-insights/culture-for-a-digital-age

Güntner, A., & Sperling, J. (2017). 'How to nudge your way to better performance'. Mckinsey Organization blog.

Heifetz, R., Grashow, A., & Linsky, M. (2009). *The Practice of Adaptive Leadership: Tools and Tactics for Changing Your Organization and the World.* Boston, Massachusetts: Harvard Business School Publishing.

Huy, Q. (2014, August 01). In Praise of Middle Managers. Retrieved December 11, 2020, from https://hbr.org/2001/09/in-praise-of-middle-manager

Kegan, R., & Laskow, L. (2001). The Real Reason People Won't Change. *Harvard Business Review*, Nov 2001.

Keller, S. (2011). *Beyond performance: How great organizations build ultimate competitive advantage.* Hoboken, N.J.: Wiley.

Kotter, J. P., & Cohen, D. S. (2012). *The heart of change: Real-life stories of how people change their organizations.* Boston, MA: Harvard Business Review Press.

Linos E., Reinhard J. (2015). A Head for Hiring: The Behavioural Science of Recruitment and Selection. Chartered Institute for Professional Development (CIPD) Research Report.

Mezias, J. M., Grinyer, P., & Guth, W. D. (2001). Changing collective cognition: A process model for strategic change. *Long Range Planning*, 34, 71–95.

Satell, G. (2019). *Cascades: How to create a movement that drives transformational change.* New York: McGraw-Hill Education.

Schein, H. (1990). Organizational Culture, *American Psychologist*, Vol.45, No.2, 109-119.

Taylor, C. (2015). *Walking the talk: Building a culture for success.* London: Random House Business Books.

Thaler, R. H., & Sunstein, C. R. (2008). *Nudge: Improving decisions using the architecture of choice.* New Haven, CT: Yale University Press.

van Essenberg, W., & Vercaeren, G. (2019). Survey results: The 'attitude' challenge of your hiring process – and 3 things you can do about it.

Westra, H., & Aviram, A. (2013). Core Skills in Motivational Interviewing. *Psychotherapy* 50(3), 273-278.

Humanizing LEADERSHIP

A HUMAN-centred approach to inspire
and create commitment to the strategy
from within the organization

'Mastering others is strength;
mastering yourself is true power.'
– Lao Tzu

**Why do people
in my organization
not engage with
the vision I shared?**

What if I could inspire
and create commitment
to the strategy from
within the organization?

Why it matters

When I look back at the companies I have worked for and the many projects I have led over the past 25 years, I have experienced good and bad examples showing the link between effective leadership and realizing strategies successfully or business performance overall. Although the type of leadership required varies and depends on the context, I am convinced that there is a strong correlation. Effective leadership increases value by driving performance.

If the leadership dimension is not properly in place, a company simply cannot be successful

A McKinsey study reveals that leadership effectiveness matters directly to organizational performance and health and is a predictor of future performance. Companies with top-quartile leadership effectiveness have on average a 3.5 times greater total return to shareholders (TRS) than companies with bottom-quartile scores, over a three-year period.

My perspective on leadership entails four critical components: (1) creating a vision and hope (2) building, motivating and inspiring teams (3) execution in terms of decision making, judging, handling crises and (4) 'walking the talk', which refers to integrity and trust. For me, effective leaders are those who meet the needs of their followers, pay careful attention to group processes, calm anxieties, arouse hope and aspirations and know how to liberate human energy and inspire people to positive actions.

One change in the behaviour of a leader might trigger a significant impact on business performance

Every day, throughout organizations, leaders make many decisions; these decisions involve interactions; and each of these can either support or harm the main effort of the organization. Because of the role modelling dimension of leadership, the impact of the behaviour of one single leader on the whole organization can be huge in a positive or negative sense.

A story to tell: Uncomfortable reflections

When I started up my consulting and coaching business, B15, I had my doubts about whether I wanted to position individual leadership coaching as one of the core service offerings to our clients. I thought I could have more impact by focusing on interventions at organizational and team level. At that time, my assumption was that the business case for individual leadership coaching (outcomes versus investment) was too unclear.

Soon, I discovered the opposite. I was in contact with CEOs and senior executives unwilling to exercise authority, micro-managing, avoiding conflicts, being inaccessible or playing (political) games. I experienced first-hand that the positive and negative impact of leadership behaviour on the performance of their teams and entire organizations was significant.

Anna hoped personal coaching would help Jamie to become more effective in her role as leader

It all started with an interesting, trusted relationship I had built up with Anna, a senior executive of a division in a company in full growth and expansion. Anna contacted me to talk about Jamie, a team leader in her leadership team, because she believed Jamie might benefit from individual coaching. Anna thought there might be a good fit between Jamie and myself for this. After our initial discussion, Anna introduced me to Felix, the HR business partner of her division, to further align on approach and to make some initial contractual arrangements.

Because leadership coaching was something new in this organization, I proposed a coaching approach starting with an intake session (chemistry check between coach and coachee) followed by five individual coaching sessions. We decided that based on the need, additional coaching sessions could be added.

> *Jamie told me about a recent painful experience and her frustration at being treated unfairly*

As a next step, I scheduled the intake meeting with Jamie. During this meeting, we talked about many different personal and professional topics like career history, recent events that had impacted her profoundly, challenges she was facing and a first discussion on leadership development areas. Jamie shared a recent painful experience where she felt that she had been treated unfairly. A few months before we met, Jamie received strong feedback about her (too) direct communication style. This feedback was a total surprise to her. She thought her direct communication style was very much appreciated and valued by her colleagues. The feedback was given in such a way that she thought she would be fired if she did not make rapid progress. I felt that Jamie was still suffering and very emotional about these recent events. She felt frustrated, and unfairly treated on the matter, but her language indicated that she was making a mindshift; she started to realize that she could learn from it and become better as a leader.

> *The language she used indicated a shift from being frustrated towards willingness to reflect and learn*

During the coaching sessions, Jamie became more aware of her functioning in general and as a leader. The in-depth discussions and reflections kept going. We used different quantitative (e.g. surveys) and qualitative (e.g. drawings and images) approaches, which helped her to gain insights about her own behaviour, the root cause behind her behaviour and its impact on her own performance and on the performance of her team. Her reflections triggered insights on her motivational drivers and the way she relates to others both inside and outside the work environment. She started to better understand what she did, why she did it and its impact.

Jamie found it challenging and had to learn to reflect about herself. Reflection is not part of the dominant logic in professional life. Most of us are wired to take action and reflection is seen as standing still and might be perceived as a weakness. The value of 'reflection time' is often doubted and mostly not associated with performance.

> *Reflection was not part of her dominant logic and felt somewhat uncomfortable*

To keep the reflection going between the coaching sessions, I asked Jamie to send me a short note of her reflections (whatever came to mind) one week after each session. At the end of each session, we also agreed on some specific actions to be taken and experimented with. In period of a few months, Jamie transitioned towards being a more effective leader, which was noticed by the people she worked with.

Based on real-life cases (often starting from a frustration) and confirmed by 360° feedback conducted on twelve general leadership competencies, it became clear that emotional intelligence (impulse control in particular) and being able to apply different communication styles were important development areas for Jamie. It also became clear that Jamie's ability to identify, control and recognize emotions, both in herself and, to an extent, in others, was an area of development. She was also struggling to recognize, understand and regulate her own emotions and to interpret the emotional responses of others.

> *Her level of self-awareness was low, especially on emotional dimensions*

Based on these insights, we reflected a lot on how Jamie was feeling and wanted to feel by selecting images that best represented her emotional state. For example, the picture opposite was selected to represent how she felt during one of the coaching sessions. The associations made were tired, confused, low energy, difficult to manage work/life, low energy, lacking control.

Picture selected representing how Jamie feels
(METALOG emotion cards)

As an example, the picture below was selected to represent how she would like to be and feel: Joy, having fun, less fights, freedom, having control.

Picture selected representing how Jamie would like to be
(METALOG emotion cards)

Jamie became more aware of what held her back from change and further growth as a leader

The coaching discussions were based on real-life situations that she had experienced. In preparation for each coaching session, I asked her to describe one or more recent, concrete situations that she was closely involved in (actor), where she was not satisfied with the result and would have wanted to change her approach. Based on these cases and with the use of some mental tools, we conducted introspective exercises to better understand the hidden forces holding her back from change and doing things differently.

She kept collecting feedback on progress from people around her that she trusted

During the final coaching session, we discussed the following questions: What is the most important thing you have learned about yourself during the coaching sessions? Where do you feel that you have become more effective? What helped with this? Where do you feel you can grow even further? What do you propose to do to ensure that you continue to grow in these areas?

I also asked for feedback on how she experienced my coaching and identification of areas of development. She responded that she appreciated my listening, not being judgmental, pushing back when needed, giving my opinion and the high level of personalization of the coaching.

I realized there is a limit to what you can reach with coaching. For me, the focus and value of coaching is to trigger a critical shift in mindset that is relevant to the context of the leader. Often more knowledge and skills building (such as stakeholder management, coaching and giving feedback) are needed to develop the leader and different formats are more appropriate to deal with these challenges (for example, deep dive training or in combination with team coaching).

The individual coaching led to team coaching interventions

The positive impact of this first coaching in the company was also noticed by Anna and Felix. This led to requests for additional coaching, mainly for employees starting in new or challenging leadership roles, key people requiring accelerated leadership development, or leaders with dysfunctional leadership behavioural patterns. We were also asked to bring in our deep expertise in leadership team coaching interventions for some strategic projects and in mitigating tensions between key people within the company.

Three HUMAN-centred tactics

In the section below, I want to share three human-centred tactics that I found to be highly impactful for increasing effectiveness as a leader:

1. Develop reflective leaders who are more aware of their own emotions and functioning.
2. Explore and articulate what you do, why you do it and the impact on performance.
3. Invest in understanding what holds you back from (further) developing as a leader.

Below I elaborate on each of the three human-centred tactics in more detail.

TACTIC 1:
Develop reflective leaders who are more aware of their own emotions and functioning

Leaders today must cultivate the ability to act seamlessly in different dimensions: forward-vision thinking, tactical execution and self-awareness. I experience that this latter ability, to think at the dimension of the self, is often underexposed by leaders.

Self-awareness of leaders is often low, especially on the emotional dimension

Most leaders have some level of awareness about their development areas. What I often experience is a lack of understanding between what they do, why they do it (root cause) and the impact of their behaviours. Exploring yourself more extensively is an essential starting point in creating greater awareness of your emotions and functioning as a leader. I learned that starting with a situation of frustration is an easy, low entry point for starting personal reflections. This exploration is the basis for potential shift, a tipping point for change, doing things differently.

Reflection is not part of the dominant logic in our lives

Reflection is not a practice that is commonly applied and promoted in most organizations today and in society in general. I assume that the value of 'reflection time' might be doubted because it does not lead to immediate action or results and is not associated with performance. During team coaching and individual coaching sessions, I often find that people do not have the habit of reflection and feel uncomfortable with it.

The language used at the start of a coaching journey indicates the intrinsic willingness to reflect and learn

A first reflection I trigger at the start of any coaching journey is the reason for the coaching. Why do you want to be coached? This is an interesting question to ask at the start of a coaching or leadership development journey. Two answers I often hear are: I want to intrinsically grow and develop as a leader, or the company has asked me to participate in the leadership development journey. Needless to say, there are many variants in between these two extremes. The answer to this question is an important indicator in understanding their willingness to learn and develop as a leader. Other clarifying questions are: How would you evaluate your functioning as a leader today on a scale of 1 to 10? What is the score you are aiming for? What is missing? Another interesting indicator of willingness to change is the language used related to who it is that needs to change: the others or me?

TACTIC 2

Explore and articulate what you do, why you do it and its impact on performance

The objective of the coaching intervention is to make leaders more effective in their specific context. It is a process of exploration and discovery of insights combined with taking practical action and learning (trying out new things). I typically apply combined qualitative and quantitative approaches, which are mainly based on INSEAD and The Tavistock Institute research, complemented by methods from Barrett Values Centre and Coaches Training Institute.

⋮ *There is no silver bullet*

Below, you will find examples of proven methods and tools I often use to create awareness and insights on intrapersonal and interpersonal dynamics impacting the functioning of the leader. Based on discussion and reflection, they trigger insights that might lead to awareness and changes in behaviours. It is important to bring different perspectives to the discussion; some tools will resonate more than others depending on the preferences and profile of the leader. There is no silver bullet; awareness arises by exploring intrapersonal (yourself) and interpersonal territories (how you relate to others) in different ways. The goal of the exploration is to trigger critical shifting points that will increase their effectiveness in their context.

EXPLORE YOURSELF

Different approaches can be used to explore yourself. Below, you will find examples of approaches I often use to start the discovery of intrapersonal dynamics, why they happen and their impact on the performance of the leader, his/her team and organization. Examples of questions asked to start the exploration are: How do you see yourself? What is important to you?

Question: How do you see yourself?

I often ask leaders to draw a self-portrait, a picture of how the leader sees himself/herself as it relates to what was in his/her head, heart, stomach, past, present, work, and leisure. Drawing provides an enormous amount of rich data about yourself. Its power resides in its capacity to give simple expression to complex feelings and ideas, and to trigger awareness and insights on the current self-image of the leader.

Example of a self-portrait of a leader

The picture above is the self-portrait made by a leader I coached. The drawing represents her in three different moments (in the past, on the left; today, in the middle; and in future, on the right). We discovered that independence and being able to speak up (from the gut) are important to her. The picture on the right also represents her boss and mentor who she appreciates, looks up to and is a real role model overall. She feels she is developing and her ambition is to become like her boss (her role model).

Question: What is important to you?

Barrett's Personal Values Assessment is an interesting and easy-to-use tool that triggers awareness and insights on the personal values of the leader. Personal values reflect what is important to us. They are a shorthand way of describing our individual motivations. Together with our beliefs, they are an important factor that drives how we act and behave.

Jamie's Personal Values Assessment report based on the ten personal values she selected was a good starting point for the discussion. The values that best represent Jamie are: accountability, courage, efficiency, family, friendship, openness, reliability, respect, trust and fairness. Trust, openness, and fairness are the three values she selected that represent her most.

The report revealed that having close relationships and connections with others is important to Jamie. She needs to feel a sense of love and belonging. If these needs are threatened or not met, she will experience anxiety about not being accepted or not being loved enough.

Based on the values selected, we also discussed that:

· Having meaningful close relationships with others is important in her life and is central in the decisions Jamie makes.
· Jamie is dependable and takes ownership of her actions so others know they can count on her.
· Building confidence with others by being receptive to others' contributions enables her to foster transparency in her interactions.
· Jamie has the strength to face her fears and to speak up even when things may be difficult.
· She likes to be effective in her endeavours and make the best use of her time.
· She strives to show consideration to others and wants to feel that this same courtesy is extended to her.
· Jamie enjoys working with others and likes to cooperate and share experiences.

Understanding our values helps us better understand ourselves and why we act or react the way we do. For example, if someone undermines one of Jamie's values, it can result in feelings of hurt; she would be likely to feel upset if her values of fairness, openness, and respect are not honoured by someone else. Remember that this is exactly what happened when Jamie received strong feedback about her direct communication style. She felt frustrated and unfairly treated, and was suffering and felt very emotional about it.

Similarly, if she makes decisions that go against one of her values, this may lead her to feel uneasy or unsettled, because she has not been true to herself.

PAUSE FOR INSIGHTS
Digital-in-the-mind of the CEO

We talked before about the fact that leaders make many decisions; these decisions involve interactions; and each of these can either support or harm the main effort of the organization. We also said that because of the role modelling dimension of leadership, the impact of the behaviour of one single leader on the whole organization can be huge in a positive or negative sense.

Saskia Van Uffelen, Digital Champion Belgium and I conducted a study in 2019 to understand 'Digital-in-the-mind of the CEO'.

'Digital-in-the-mind of the ceo' is defined as his/her representation of digitalization, being a subjective, emotional reality, self-constructed images of digitalization. These mental representations give rise to thoughts, images, emotions that influence their behaviour, facilitating or impeding the successful implementation of digitalization. We strongly believe that the CEO's behaviour significantly impacts the success of implementing digital agendas in organizations.

In this study we wanted to map the digital readiness of Belgian organizations and share thoughts, practices, critical success factors and challenges to make them (more) digital ready. We interviewed Belgian CEOs from very diverse sectors and types of organization in order to get their perspectives on this. We talked to leaders from Small & Medium business in building, manufacturing, insurance, academia, and hospital, security and industrial sectors.

The approach we took combined quantitative and qualitative methods. During interviews we asked the CEOs to select a picture (from the internet) or to make a drawing that represents digitalization for you. Examples of associations made were: fun, free time, connected, uberization, footprint, being watched (big brother), opportunity to co-create, breaking silos, need interdisciplinarity, exciting heydays, takes effort, abstract, disruption, self-driving car, social/ethical (bigger gap), sharing economy, client-centricity, etc.

Images selected by the CEOs interviewed representing digitalization
(METALOG emotion cards)

We also asked them to complete a short survey and discussed and reflected on a number of questions: How successful is your board in realizing its digital agenda? How successful is your leadership team in realizing its digital agenda? How successful is your organization in realizing its digital agenda? How successful are you (as CEO) in realizing the digital agenda?

My board...	Average score
understands **why** digital is important	4,4
wants to **make digital agenda happen** in my organization	4,2
believes our story about digital	4,0
sees the urgency to digital in my organization	3,4
feels **capable** to realize digital agenda in my organization	3,3
has the **knowledge** to realize digital agenda	2,8

■ High (3.75 and above)   ■ Medium (3.25 to 3.74)   ■ Low (less than 3.25)

Results: How successful is your board in realizing its digital agenda?
(as perceived by the CEOs interviewed)

I (as CEO)...	Average score
understand **why** digital is important	4,8
believe our story about digital	4,8
want to **make digital agenda happen** in my organization	4,7
see the urgency to digital in my organization	4,7
have the **knowledge** to realize digital agenda	3,6
feel **capable** to realize digital agenda in my organization	3,3

■ High (3.75 and above)   ■ Medium (3.25 to 3.74)   ■ Low (less than 3.25)

Results: How successful are you (as CEO) in realizing the digital agenda?
(as perceived by the CEOs interviewed)

The picture below gives a consolidated perspective on scores given by the CEOs with regard to the overall success in realizing the digital agenda.

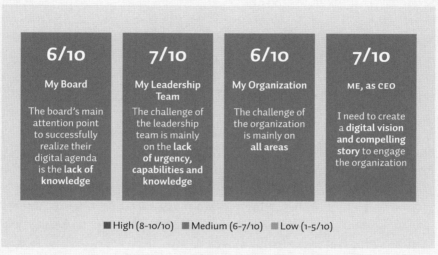

6/10	7/10	6/10	7/10
My Board	**My Leadership Team**	**My Organization**	ME, AS CEO
The board's main attention point to successfully realize their digital agenda is the **lack of knowledge**	The challenge of the leadership team is mainly on the **lack of urgency, capabilities and knowledge**	The challenge of the organization is mainly on **all areas**	I need to create a **digital vision and compelling story** to engage the organization

■ High (8-10/10)   ■ Medium (6-7/10)   ■ Low (1-5/10)

Consolidated perspective on success in realizing the digital agenda
(as perceived by the CEOs interviewed)

> *The 'digital' challenges in the mind of CEOs are related to the sense of urgency, knowledge and capabilities.*

Our study revealed some interesting findings. Overall, digitalization is perceived by the CEOs interviewed as something positive and not threatening; the (upcoming) era of technological heydays creates interesting opportunities. 65% of the CEOs interviewed have a cautious approach to digital disruption (digitalization) based on small initiatives.

The CEOs interviewed consider themselves (as CEO) and the leadership team as 'averagely' successful in realizing the digital agenda. The board and organization are considered as less successful. Key challenges are related to the sense of urgency, the lack of knowledge and capabilities to realize the digital agenda.

Digitalization also requires more radical customer-centricity, co-creation with customers. CEOs also mention the importance to better co-create internally, to break down silos between departments and combine multi-disciplinary, transversal forces within the organization.

Strategic alliances and teamwork are the most critical values to realize the digital agenda. The values continuous learning and customer satisfaction are 'needed more' by the highest percentage of CEOs to make the realization of the digital agenda a success. Finally, digitalization is seen as a continuous change process. The key challenges are mostly people related, requiring a fundamental shift in mindset and continuous learning.

PAUSE FOR THOUGHT
Explore and discover 'Digital-in-your-mind'

1. Select a picture (from the internet) or make a drawing that represents digitalization for you. Write down the associations, thoughts, feelings you make about this picture or drawing.
2. Answer the following questions: How successful is your board in realizing its digital agenda? How successful is your leadership team in realizing its digital agenda? How successful is your organization in realizing its digital agenda? How successful are you (as CEO) in realizing the digital agenda?

   For each of the questions, think about:

   · understanding why digital is important;
   · willingness to make the digital agenda happen in our organization;
   · belief in the story about digitalization;
   · seeing the urgency to digital in our organization;
   · feeling capable to realize digital agenda in my organization;
   · having the knowledge to realize the digital agenda.

3. What critical values and mindset are needed in your organization to realize the digital agenda?
4. What did you discover about 'Digital-in-your-mind'? How do you think this influences your behaviour in facilitating or impeding the successful implementation of digitalization in your organization?

EXPLORE HOW YOU RELATE TO OTHERS

There are various approaches that can be used to explore how you relate to others. Below are examples of approaches I often use to start the discovery of interpersonal dynamics, why they happen and their impact on the performance of the leader, his/her team and organization. Examples of questions I ask to start the exploration are:

- How do you perform in carrying out the primary tasks of a leader?
- How well developed is your emotional and social skill set?
- How do you typically deal with conflicts?
- What is your repetitive pattern in relationship difficulties?

Question: How do you perform in carrying out the primary tasks of a leader?

The GELM® (Global Executive Leadership Mirror) is a 360° feedback survey I often use. It is designed to help executives evaluate their performance in dimensions vital to leadership success. It measures specific leadership behaviours and provides feedback across four main levels: Self, Teams, Organization and Networks. It is developed to help executives evaluate their performance in carrying out the twelve primary tasks of global leaders.

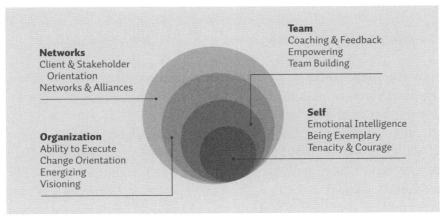

12 leadership behaviour competencies grouped across four levels
(Source: Global Executive Leadership Mirror by Kets de Vries Institute)

The graph below represents Jamie's leadership strengths and development areas on these four levels and twelve leadership competencies. The upper line represents Jamie's self-assessment on these twelve competencies; the lower line represents the evaluation by the observers she identified. The graph shows that Jamie consistently overestimates herself and that she scores high on tenacity and courage and being exemplary, but rather low on emotional intelligence, visioning, change orientation, client and stakeholder orientation and networking and alliances. This picture created a solid basis for discussion on her leadership strengths and development areas.

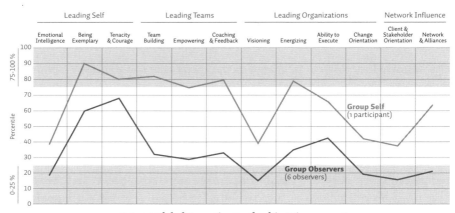

Extract Global Executive Leadership Mirror report
(Source: Global Executive Leadership Mirror by Kets de Vries Institute)

Question: How developed are your emotional and social skills?

A more in-depth focus on Emotional Intelligence is often valuable as it is a dimension missing in many organizations. Ilham Kadri, CEO of Solvay, argues that Intelligence is becoming a commodity, but what is rare is Emotional Intelligence. She defines Emotional Intelligence as never being afraid of going to your peers or bosses to suggest changes, never being afraid to dare to play the game or to hire someone who is smarter than you. She says that you decide each day which kind of person you want to be. We can care and dare; they are not in opposition and you can have both. Do not get stuck in some old practice just because that's the way it has always been. Get rid of it, there's always an opportunity to do better!

> *Intelligence is becoming a commodity, but what is rare is Emotional Intelligence*

Emotional Intelligence is a set of emotional and social skills that influence the way we perceive and express ourselves, develop and maintain social relationships, cope with challenges, and use emotional information in an effective and meaningful way. It is proven to be a key indicator of human performance and development. People who are higher in Emotional Intelligence communicate effectively, form strong relationships, and create powerful coping strategies. Emotional Intelligence can be measured – more accessibly and less controversially than IQ – and unlike IQ, it can be substantially strengthened and developed.

> *Emotional Intelligence is proven to be a key indicator of human performance and development*

The Emotional Quotient Inventory 2.0 (EQ-i 2.0) is a scientifically validated Emotional Intelligence tool that I often use. It measures an individual's emotional intelligence based on a 133-question self-assessment that explores the frequency and role that sixteen different elements of emotional well-being play in your life. Through extensive research, the following five scales make up the key dimensions of this assessment: self-perception, self-expression, interpersonal, decision making, and stress management.

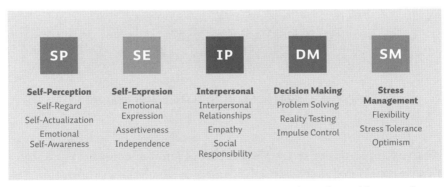

The five scales of Emotional Intelligence (Source: EQ-i 2.0 by Multi-Health Systems)

The EQ-i 2.0 assessment tool provides an overall Emotional Intelligence score with five composite scores measuring five distinct aspects of emotional and social functioning. Fifteen sub-scales home in on Emotional Intelligence skills critical to workplace success (see picture below). Also, a well-being indicator measures the level of happiness resulting in additional development opportunities.

The EQ-i 2.0 model (Source: EQ-i 2.0 by Multi-Health Systems)

As an example, opposite you see a subset of Jamie's scores for three scales that we considered as critical in the context in which she was operating. The results show that she scores adequate/average in terms of decision making and stress management and rather low on the interpersonal scale (interpersonal relationships, empathy and social responsibility).

Dimension: Interpersonal	84
Interpersonal Relationships Mutual satisfying relationships	(95)
Empathy Understanding, appreciating how others feel	(83)
Social Responsibility Social consciousness; helpful	(83)

Dimension: Decision Making	104
Problem Solving Find solutions when emotions are involved	(112)
Reality Check Objective; see things as they really are	(102)
Impulse Control Resist or delay impulse to act	(97)

Dimension: Stress Management	107
Flexibility Adapting emotions, thoughts and behaviours	(119)
Stress Tolerance Coping with stressful situations	(108)
Optimism Positive attitude and outlook on life	(91)

■ Very high (+120) ■ High (110-119) ■ Adequate/Average (90-109) ■ Low (80-89) ■ Very low (-80)

Example of results of Emotional Intelligence scores (Source: EQ-i 2.0 by Multi-Health Systems)

Question: How do you typically deal with conflicts?

The Thomas-Kilmann Conflict Mode Instrument (TKI) assesses an individual's behaviour in conflict situations – that is, situations in which the concerns of two people appear to be incompatible. In conflict situations, we can describe a person's behaviour along two basic dimensions:

- Assertiveness, the extent to which the individual attempts to satisfy his or her own concerns, and
- Cooperativeness, the extent to which the individual attempts to satisfy the other person's concerns.

These two dimensions of behaviour can be used to define five methods of dealing with conflict. In the case of conflict-handling behaviour, there are no right or wrong answers. All five modes are useful in some situations: each represents a set of useful social skills. You are capable of using all five conflict-handling modes; you cannot be characterized as having a single, rigid style of dealing with conflict. However, I experience that most people use some modes more readily than others, develop more skills in those modes, and therefore tend to rely on them more heavily. Many have a clear favourite.

The diagram below shows Jamie's scores and profile:

- Collaborating: 8
- Compromising: 7
- Competing: 6
- Accommodating: 5
- Avoiding: 4

Jamie's profile shows that in situations of conflict, she can apply different styles, which is an asset in effectively dealing with conflicts (if she applies them consciously).

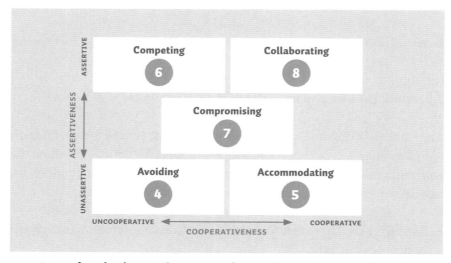

Extract from the Thomas Kilmann report (Source: Thomas-Kilmann conflict mode instrument by Thomas & Kilmann)

Question: What is your repetitive pattern in relationship difficulties?

The three most common leadership dysfunctions I see are (1) unwillingness to exercise authority (2) tyrannizing subordinates and (3) micromanagement. All these can be explained by often unconscious needs that hold one back from changing this dysfunctional behaviour. Unwillingness to exercise authority often reflects the underlying need to be liked. Tyrannizing subordinates often reflects the underlying need to get even and micromanagement, the underlying need to be perfect.

The Core Conflictual Relationship Theme is at the heart of all repetitive relationship difficulties

There is an important but more complex dynamic behind this, which is called CCRT, Core Conflictual Relationship Theme. I will provide a basic outline of this dynamic below, but bear in mind that this is a simplified version of a more complex concept. The CCRT is based on Freud's concept of transference, which states that early interpersonal experiences predispose a person to initiate and conduct close relationships in particular ways and in a repeated fashion later in life. In other words, our expectations of other people's responses in the present are coloured by our feelings, attitudes, and behaviour towards significant people from the past ('transference'). As a result, we sometimes unconsciously tempt people in the present to respond in ways that we expect from them. Transference can cause people to replay the scripts that they have lived in the past. This core conflictual relationship theme takes hold in our personal lives and it is the heart of all repetitive relationship difficulties.

Each person's CCRT has the following three components:

1. A wish in the context of a relationship (W: Wish)
2. Our anticipation of how others will react to us in the context of this wish (RO: Reaction of Others)
3. Our own reaction to this response, be it behavioural or affective. (RS: Reaction of Self; affective, behaviour or fantasies).

How do we gain insight into our own CCRT? According to Howard E. Book, the CCRT is developed by listening for relationship episodes. The CCRT itself is generated from a number of relationship episodes told by the coachee about his or her interaction with another person. From these episodes, as coach, I extract (1) the wish, intent, or desire (W) in the context of that other person (2) his or her belief and assumptions about how the other person might respond (RO) in the context of that wish and (3) what the leader actually does (behavioural component of the RS) and feels (affective component of the RS) in the context of the anticipated response (RO).

Example of a CCRT I discovered during a leadership coaching session: From what we have been talking about, I sense that you want to be in a relationship where you feel free to speak your mind (W) – particularly when it comes to your own ideas and opinions – but you fear that, if you do so, others will think you and your ideas are silly and laughable (RO). So instead of speaking, you do not venture an opinion, but remain silent (RSb) and end up feeling extremely frustrated and self-critical (RSa).

Examples of common wishes (W) are:

·   To assert the self and be independent
·   To oppose, hurt and control others
·   To be controlled, hurt and not responsible
·   To be distant and avoid conflicts
·   To be close and accepting
·   To be loved and understood
·   To feel good and comfortable
·   To achieve and help others

Examples of common responses (RO) from others are:

·   Strong
·   Controlling
·   Upset
·   Bad

- Rejecting and opposing
- Helpful
- Likes me
- Understanding

Examples of common responses of self (RS) are:

- Helpful
- Unreceptive
- Respected and accepted
- Oppose and hurt others
- Self-controlled and self-confident
- Helpless
- Disappointed and depressed
- Anxious and ashamed

It is important to manage the CCRT, not necessarily change it. Here, manage means put it into words, make it more accurate, become aware of it, bring it out of the dark into the light.

> *It enhances self-awareness because you become aware of your conflicts, wishes, desires, fears, anxieties, biases, prejudices, assumptions, and blind spots*

When the CCRT has been discovered, the focus can be put on managing it. Try to identify and attempt to actualize the wish (W); simultaneously, identify and attempt to inhibit the RS and contain and 'deal with' the RO as a transference distortion. Where is the evidence? What would you suggest to a colleague who came to you with the same difficulty? How is this related to your relationship with your parents?

Invest in understanding what holds you back from (further) developing as a leader

Apart from the awareness of the functioning as a leader, there is another important awareness that needs to be triggered during coaching: awareness about the way you learn, change your behaviour and, more importantly, what holds you back from learning and making a personal change.

The dynamics of individual change often start from daily frustration

Manfred Kets de Vries argues that preparatory work leading to cognitive, affective, and behavioural reframing of situations is essential to effecting tipping point moments. He believes there is a sequence that leads up to 'Aha!' moments, beginning with frustration. When leaders undergoing coaching become more aware of this frustration and acknowledge it, tipping points are on the rise. Tipping points grow out of thinking and reflection.

Let's start by looking at the five Cs of change. These are the necessary components of any individual change process.

The five Cs are:

1. **C**oncern about present, unpleasant emotions like sadness, anger and frustration induce a reappraisal of behaviour and then change. It is about the negative emotion.
2. **C**onfrontation is a trigger for the first incremental changes. It is about the focal point.
3. **C**larification of change means making it public. You have to go through with the change once it is made public. The public declaration of intent.
4. **C**rystallization stage brings ideas and plans into definite form. It is about the inner journey.
5. It is then that the mindset shows that **C**hange has been achieved. The new mindset is internalized.

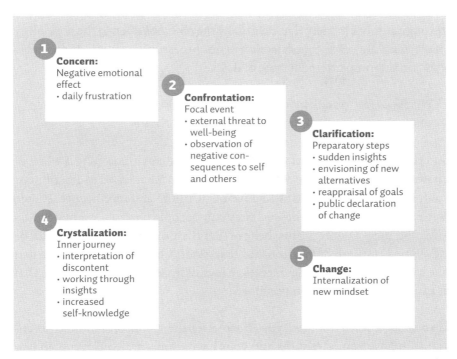

1. **Concern:**
Negative emotional effect
· daily frustration

2. **Confrontation:**
Focal event
· external threat to well-being
· observation of negative con-sequences to self and others

3. **Clarification:**
Preparatory steps
· sudden insights
· envisioning of new alternatives
· reappraisal of goals
· public declaration of change

4. **Crystalization:**
Inner journey
· interpretation of discontent
· working through insights
· increased self-knowledge

5. **Change:**
Internalization of new mindset

The five Cs of individual change (Source: The Leadership Mystique by Manfred Kets de Vries)

According to Schein, there are two kinds of anxiety associated with learning: 'learning anxiety' and 'survival anxiety'. Learning anxiety comes from being afraid to try something new for fear that it will be too difficult, that we will look stupid in the attempt, or that we will have to part from old habits that have worked for us in the past. Learning something new can cast us as the deviant in the groups we belong to. It can threaten our self-esteem and, in extreme cases, even our identity.

You cannot talk people out of their learning anxieties; they're the basis for resistance to change

You can't talk people out of their learning anxieties; they're the basis for resistance to change. And given the intensity of those fears, none of us would ever try something new unless we experienced the second form of anxiety, survival anxiety – the horrible realization that in order to make it, you're going to have to change. Learners experience so much hopelessness through survival anxiety that eventually they become open to the possibility of learning. But even this dejection is not necessarily enough. Individuals can remain in a permanent state of despair.

> *People with a growth mindset understand that effort and perseverance make them stronger, which helps them achieve more*

Another interesting insight to explore during leadership coaching is whether the leader has a fixed or growth mindset. These terms are used to describe our underlying beliefs and attitudes towards learning and intelligence. People with a 'growth mindset' believe they can become smarter, more productive, and more talented. They believe that their most basic abilities can be developed through dedication and hard work – brains and talent are just the starting point. This view creates a love of learning and a resilience that is essential for great accomplishment.

If you have a 'fixed mindset', you effectively believe you have limited potential. You have your strengths and your limitations, and you are unable to work above and beyond them. In a fixed mindset, people believe their basic qualities, like their intelligence or talent, are simply fixed traits. They spend their time documenting their intelligence or talent instead of developing this. People with a growth mindset tend to achieve more than those with a more fixed mindset. This is because they worry less about looking smart and put more energy into learning.

Fixed and growth mindsets differ in underlying beliefs and attitudes:

FIXED VERSUS GROWTH MINDSET

Intelligence is something you have or don't have	Intelligence is something you are able to develop
With a **fixed mindset** we tend to:	With a **growth mindset** we tend to:
• Avoid taking on challenges	• Embrace any challenge
• Quit or give up easily	• Never give up
• Be highly self-critical	• Practise self-compassion
• See effort as pointless	• See effort as a journey
• Disregard criticism	• Learn from all criticism
• Resent the success of others	• Be inspired by others' success
• Criticize and judge others	• Help and nurture others
• Argue for our limitations	• Believe in possibilities

Underlying beliefs and attitudes of fixed and growth mindsets (Source: Mindset by Carol Dweck)

I like to highlight three other hidden forces that I often see in action during coaching sessions and that block changing mindsets and behaviours. Below, you will find three mental tools that help to discover (bring to the surface) and deal effectively with these hidden dynamics, which play at the intrapersonal and interpersonal levels. The first two play at the intrapersonal level and are called (1) 'the authenticity paradox' and (2) 'Find your hidden competing commitment', which we discussed in chapter 3. The third one is a more complex blocker of change that plays at the interpersonal level and is called (3) CCRT (Core Conflictual Relationship Theme), the repetitive pattern in relationship difficulties, which we discussed before.

An image of self that is too rigid prevents us from experimenting and trying new approaches

When discussing personal values with leaders, I often get into a discussion on how to deal effectively with colleagues with a different set of values. This discussion leads us to the topic of authenticity. Herminia Ibarra raises the issue that people can be too authentic. That is, they stick to a rigid image of the self that can negatively impact leadership effectiveness. Authenticity is the notion of 'true self', I know who I am and have a consistent way of operating. Ibarra states that an image of the self that is rigid prevents us from experimenting and trying new approaches. She says, 'Because going against our natural inclinations can make us feel like imposters, we tend to latch on to authenticity as an excuse for sticking with what's comfortable.' Ibarra suggests that a self-image that is too rigid comes from too much introspection and only looking within for the answers.

The advice she gives is to learn from diverse role models, to experiment. This is not imitating or faking it, but taking effective elements from others and moulding these to become your own: 'To begin thinking like leaders, we must first act; plunge ourselves into new projects and activities, interact with different kinds of people, and experiment with new ways of getting things done. The only way we grow as leaders is by stretching the limits of who we are – doing new things that make us uncomfortable but teach us through direct experience who we want to become.'

Find your hidden competing commitment

Before each coaching session, I ask the coachee to think about real-life situations in their recent experience. I ask them to describe one (or more) recent, concrete situation in which he/she was closely involved (actor), where he/she was not satisfied with the result and that he/she would have wanted to approach differently. Based on these cases, we conduct introspective exercises to better understand the hidden competing commitment that makes it hard to change.

In the book *The Real Reason People Won't Change*, Kegan and Lahey show how our individual beliefs along with the collective mindsets in organizations combine to create a natural but powerful immunity to change. They assert that change is extremely difficult, be it on the personal or the organizational level, due to hidden competing commitments, big assumptions and ingrained thought patterns that discourage individuals and teams from abandoning the status quo.

Below is an example of a tool that helps to find your hidden competing commitments. The script of this mindfulness exercise is as follows:

Step 1 – Your commitment: Select a behaviour you want to change for yourself.

> *Example:*
> · I want to be more patient and listen better.

Step 2 – Doing/Not doing: What are you doing or not doing that prevents you from applying this behaviour?

> *Examples:*
> · I push issues through.
> · I get my view out first.
> · I don't connect with the person but the issue.

Step 3 – Competing commitment: What might be a worry, discomfort, something you fear if you would apply your desired behaviour?

> *Examples:*
> · I might be seen as not delivering.
> · I might not be taken seriously.
> · I might not be valued.

Step 4 – The big assumption: What is the worst thing that could happen if you applied your desired behaviour?

> *Examples:*
> · People will reject me.
> · I will be excluded and all alone.

Step 5 – Small experiment: What small steps can you take towards applying the new behaviour?

> *Example:*
> · Count to ten before saying something in a team meeting.

I hope the examples above convinced you that awareness about the way you learn, change your behaviour and, more importantly, what holds you back from learning and making a personal change is essential to further develop as leader.

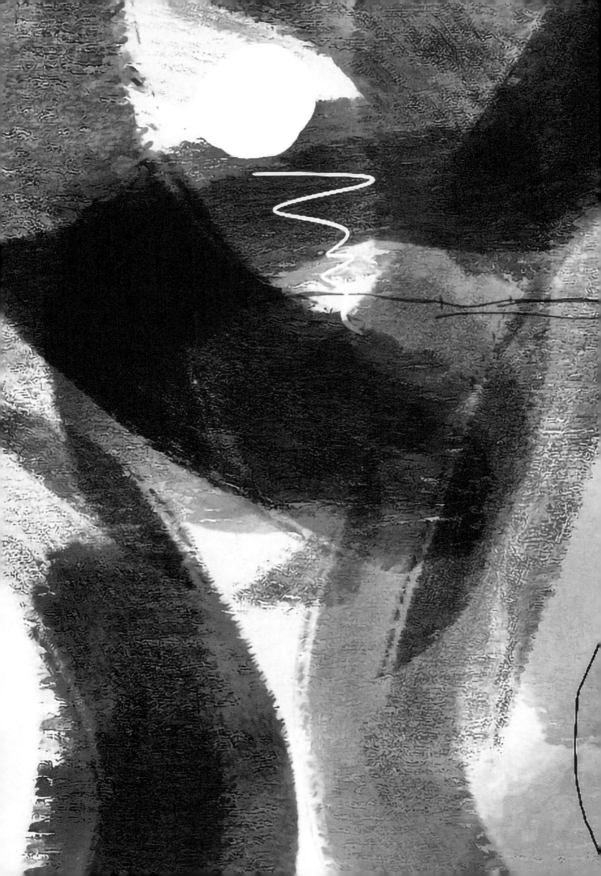

← PREVIOUS PAGES

Peter's narrative

A still, reflective Mind

A leader practises finding stillness in his
mind in a turbulent business environment.
Through reflection and self-awareness,
he is able to question and challenge himself.
This further strengthens his ability to
embrace vision and purpose in an
ambiguous and unpredictable world.

Summarizing the main points

Inspiring and creating commitment to the strategy from within the organization

- **If the leadership dimension is not properly in place, organizations simply cannot be successful.** Effective leadership matters directly in organizational performance. One change in the behaviour of a leader might trigger a significant impact on business performance in a positive or negative sense.

- **Three HUMAN-centred tactics** that I found highly impactful in increasing the effectiveness of leadership:

  1. Develop reflective leaders who are more aware of their own emotions and functioning.
  2. Explore and articulate what you do, why you do it and its impact on performance.
  3. Invest in understanding what holds you back from further developing as a leader.

- **Reflection is not part of the dominant logic in our (professional) lives.** Self-awareness is the essential starting point to trigger potential shifts in mindset and behaviour (tipping points).

- I experience that the level of **self-awareness of leaders is often low, especially on the emotional dimension.**

- **There is no silver bullet.** Creating awareness about what you do, why you do it and its impact on performance is an important first step in leadership development. Proven qualitative and quantitative methods and tools can help leaders to explore themselves and how they relate to others.

- Learning anxiety, a fixed mindset and 'competing commitments' are examples of **hidden forces holding leaders back from further growth as a leader and making personal changes.**

►How to get started

TACTIC 1
Develop reflective leaders who are more aware of their own emotions and functioning

► Reflections to get started

Please answer the questions below:

- Do you want to further develop as leader? Why?
- How effective are you today as leader on a scale from 1 to 10? What is the score you are aiming for?
- Where do you need/want to grow to become more effective as leader in your context? What is lacking in terms of knowledge, skills, mindset, behaviour to reach this level?
- What will be the impact of this growth on yourself, your team and organization?

TACTIC 2
Explore and articulate what you do, why you do it and its impact on performance

► Reflection: Explore yourself

Please draw a self-portrait.

Take a piece of paper and pens and make a drawing of yourself which includes elements of what is in your head, heart, stomach, past, present, work, and leisure.

Some drawing tips: You don't need to be an artist. There is no right or wrong. Draw whatever comes to mind. Don't think too much. Avoid words and charts. Enjoy!

Take a step back. What did you discover about yourself? What does this tell about how you look at yourself? What does the drawing tell about what is important to you?

▶ **Reflection: How developed are your emotional and social skills?**

Where do you see areas of strengths and development on the five scales of Emotional Intelligence? Please use the scales below as a reference for reflection.

- ☐ My abilities related to **self-perception**: self-regard, self-actualization, and emotional self-awareness.
- ☐ My abilities related to **self-expression**: emotional expression, assertiveness, and independence.
- ☐ My **interpersonal abilities**: interpersonal relationships, empathy, and social responsibility.
- ☐ My abilities related to **decision making**: problem solving, reality testing and impulse control.
- ☐ My abilities related to **stress management**: flexibility, stress tolerance and optimism.

(Source: The EQ-i 2.0 model – Multi-Health Systems)

What did you discover about yourself?

TACTIC 3
Invest in understanding what holds you back from (further) developing as a leader

► **Reflection: Find your hidden competing commitment.**

Step 1 – Your commitment: Select a behaviour you want to change for yourself.

Tip: Think about specific behaviours related to (1) interactions with others (2) use of time (3) decision making.

Step 2 – Doing/Not doing: What are you doing or not doing that prevents you from applying this behaviour?

Step 3 – Competing commitment: What might be a worry, discomfort, something you fear if you would apply your desired behaviour?

Tip: Think about worries related to not belonging, not being appreciated, lack of autonomy, shame or guilt.

Step 4 – The big assumption: What is the worst thing that could happen if you applied your desired?

Step 5 – Small experiment: What small steps can you take towards applying the new behaviour?

▶ **Reflection: Do you have a growth or fixed mindset?**

Please select one statement by row, which resonates most with you:

Column A	Column B
☐ Intelligence is something you have or don't have	☐ Intelligence is something you can develop
☐ I tend to avoid taking on challenges	☐ I tend to embrace any challenge
☐ I tend to quit or give up easily	☐ I tend to never give up
☐ I tend to be highly self-critical	☐ I tend to practise self-compassion
☐ I tend to see effort as pointless	☐ I tend to see effort as a journey
☐ I tend to disregard criticism	☐ I tend to learn from criticism
☐ I tend to resent the success of others	☐ I tend to be inspired by others' success
☐ I tend to criticize and judge others	☐ I tend to help and nurture others
☐ I tend to argue for our limitations	☐ I tend to believe in possibilities

Count the number of times you have selected column A and B. Look at your total scores. Column A represents a fixed mindset, column B, a growth mindset.

▶ **What did you learn? What are you going to do next?**

....

....

....

....

....

Good luck!

'I've learned that people will forget what you said, people will forget what you did, but people will never forget how you made them feel.'

– Maya Angelou

Chapter 4: **Key references and interesting reads**

Book, Howard E., & Stein, Steven J. (2011). *The EQ Edge: Emotional Intelligence and Your Success*, San Francisco, US: Jossey-Bass.

Coutu, D. (2002, March 01). The anxiety of learning. Interview Edgar H. Schein by Diane L. Coutu. Retrieved December, 2020, from https://hbr.org/2002/03/the-anxiety-of-learning

Dweck, C. (2016, January 13). What Having a 'Growth Mindset' Actually Means. Retrieved August 06, 2020, from https://hbr.org/2016/01/what-having-a-growth-mindset-actually-means

Dweck, C. S. (2017). *Mindset: Changing the way you think to fulfil your potential*. New York: Robinson.

Emotional Quotient Inventory (EQ-i 2.0). (n.d.). Retrieved August 06, 2020, from https://b15.be/we-are-eq-i-2-0-eq-360-certified/

Feser, Claudio, Rennie, Michael, & Nielsen, Nicolai Chen. (2019). *Leadership at Scale Better leadership, better results*. Place of publication not identified: Hachette Books Ireland.

Gardner, H. (2011). *Frames of mind: The theory of multiple intelligences*. New York, NY: Basic Books.

Gladwell, M. (2015). *The tipping point: How little things can make a big difference*. London: Abacus.

Grant, A. (2014). *Give and take: A revolutionary approach to success*. London: Weidenfeld & Nicolson.

Ibarra, H. (2015). *Act like a leader, think like a leader*. Boston (Massachusetts): Harvard Business Review Press.

Kegan, R., & Laskow, L. (2001). The Real Reason People Won't Change. *Harvard Business Review*, Nov 2001.

Kets de Vries, Manfred F. R. (2009). *Sex, money, happiness, and death: Musings from the underground*. Basingstoke: Palgrave Macmillan.

Kets de Vries, M.F. R. (2001). *The leadership mystique: A user's manual for the human enterprise*. Harlow: Financial Times Prentice Hall.

Kohlrieser, G. (2006). *Hostage at the table: How leaders can overcome conflict, influence others, and raise performance*. San Francisco: Jossey-Bass.

Manzoni, J., & Barsoux, J. (2003). *The set-up-to-fail-syndrome: How good managers cause great people to fail*. Boston, MA: Harvard Business School Press.

Schein, E. H., & Schein, P. A. (2018). *Humble leadership: The power of relationships, openness, and trust.* Oakland: Berrett-Koehler.

Stein, S. J. (2017). *The EQ leader: Instilling passion, creating shared goals, and building meaningful organizations through emotional intelligence.* Somerset: Wiley.

Strelecky, J. P. (2010). *The big five for life: A story of one man and leadership's greatest secret.* London: Piatkus.

Take a Look at Yourself in the Leadership Mirror. (n.d.). Retrieved August 06, 2020, from https://www.kdvi.com/research_items/851

Thomas, K. W., Kilmann, R. H. (2007). *Thomas-Kilmann conflict mode instrument.* Mountain View, CA: CPP.

Humanizing future-proof
ORGANIZATIONS

A HUMAN-centred approach to building future-proof organizations

'You can't connect the dots looking forward; you can only connect them looking backward. So, you have to trust that the dots will somehow connect in your future.'

– Steve Jobs

**Why is my organization
not ready to deal
effectively with rapidly
changing challenges?**

YOUR **HOPE**

**What if I could build
a future-proof organization
based on efficiency,
values, trust and fun?**

Why it matters

We are inefficient, too rigid, too complex, too costly, with too many conflicts and politics or disengagement, people don't feel well, stressed and there is a lack of pride or fun among employees. These are examples of frustrations and concerns I often hear when I talk to leaders about their organization.

The underlying question or concern is often: Will we be able to deal with the rapidly changing challenges or, even more fundamentally, will we stay relevant in the future and survive? A client I worked with recently defined being 'future-proof' as anticipating the future and having the ability to maximize potential and minimize the shocks and stresses of future events. The environment organizations operate in will only continue to become more unpredictable and complex. They are in a near permanent state of organizational flux.

Organizations today live in a context of increased complexity, uncertainty, and continuous change

A study of The Boston Consulting Group on the internal operations of more than 100 US and European companies confirms this trend of increased complexity. They found that the number of procedures, vertical layers, interface structures, coordination bodies, and decision approvals within organizations had increased by anywhere from 50% to 350% over a 15-year period, in response to growing external complexity. The key question is how effectively do these organizations deal with this increased external complexity internally?

Traditional organizational models cannot keep up

In this era of exponential change, traditional organizational models cannot keep up. Business today is largely structured the same way it has been for a century. In my experience, today's management systems, structures and talent strategies tend to be outdated and are designed for an era when size and enduring stability defined competitive advantage.

How future work is organized within organizations and within broader ecosystems is a significant accelerator in the performance of organizations. It significantly impacts value creation, staying relevant, and survival.

The good news is that many organizations are currently reinventing their organization or implementing new organizational models. For example, they might operate as empowered networks that are coordinated through culture, information systems, and talent mobility (Team of Teams). These organizational models set minimal boundaries, clarity and structure (in terms of vision, desired behaviours and so on), and this is combined with the empowerment and creativity of employees within these boundaries.

PAUSE FOR INSIGHTS
Mental health and well-being

I believe that organizations have a key role to play in supporting employees' mental health and well-being. Humanizing your strategy has an impact on the mental health and well-being of employees; it supports people to stay well at work.

Mental health and well-being describe our mental state – how we are feeling and how well we can cope with day-to-day life. Mental health is defined by the WHO as a state of mental and psychological well-being in which every individual realizes his or her own potential, can cope with the normal stresses of life, can work productively and fruitfully, and is able to make a contribution to his or her community. It is determined by a range of socioeconomic, biological and environmental factors. Poor mental health impacts individuals' overall health, their ability to work productively (if at all), their relationships with others, and societal costs related to unemployment, poor workplace productivity and health and social care.

Mental well-being is defined by the UK Department of Health as feeling good and functioning well and comprises each individual's experience of their life and a comparison of life circumstances with social norms and values. If employees have good mental well-being they are able to feel relatively confident in themselves and have positive self-esteem, feel and express a range of emotions, build and maintain good relationships with others, feel engaged with the world around them, live and work productively and adapt and manage in times of change and uncertainty.

It is important to raise the priority given to this in order to move towards a culture that proactively manages mental well-being. The COVID-19 pandemic might have triggered a tipping point on this matter.

A story to tell: Speed, Gears and Brakes

'It feels like we are driving at 120 km/hour in second gear,' were the first words from the company CHRO, Victoria, when we first met. 'This does not feel comfortable and it feels like something is holding us back to move forward and grow.' Victoria asked me if I could help by bringing my expertise, insights, and perspective on how to transition towards a future-proof organization that supported their growth plans.

Something is holding us back

During the next meeting with Victoria, the COO and CEO, we discussed their growth ambitions and plans in detail. We also discussed the challenges they encountered in depth: they brought up the inefficiencies within the organization and the high level of stress among employees. Initially we thought of focusing only on the leadership team, but after some discussion, we decided to position the initiative as a company-wide project involving everyone in the organization. We also agreed to focus on the visible technical organizational elements such as structure, roles, governance, leadership, process and tools. Simultaneously, we would tap into their world of values, beliefs, emotions and the underlying motivational forces influencing the individual and collective behaviour within the organization.

An organization-wide initiative to become future-proof was launched

During an informal town hall session, Victoria and I jointly introduced the project and explained how we planned to involve all employees in this exercise. I explained the two central questions we wanted to get answers to: How can we increase efficiency? How do we create a workplace where employees continue to feel good and engaged? As a next step, I invited all employees to complete a survey, which was sent to them right after the town hall session. I also invited them to have a one-on-one discussion with me, if they were interested. During the town hall session, there was little reaction; it was hard for me to find out what they were thinking about this initiative.

Exploring the broad organizational spectrum by focusing on structural, motivational, and behavioural dimensions pays off

The analysis was started by sending a survey to the whole organization to get broad insights on the strengths and points of improvement of the organization. The organizational spectrum we wanted to cover and evaluate was broad; we focused on employee engagement, loyalty, stress and well-being, increased structural efficiency and effectiveness of the organization (in terms of decision making, coordination and so on), level of trust and psychological safety, collaboration between different teams, current and desired values, culture and behaviours, interpersonal dynamics and leadership.

Understand the work to be done and the context around it.

In parallel with the survey, I conducted one-on-one interviews with the directors of the organization, a selection of employees in key functions and employees who were interested and willing to share their experience, thoughts and insights. During these interviews, we started by discussing the clarity of the vision. Afterwards, we discussed their work and specific context. Examples of questions I asked were: What are the key activities? How do you measure success? What does a typical week look like? With whom do you interact most? What are the key challenges in your role? What are you proud of? What frustrates you? What motivates you?

Interviews are also a great way to explore the 'Organization-in-the-mind'; the subjective, emotional reality of your organization as perceived by employees, which provides critical insight on the motivational drivers and functional/ dysfunctional behaviours within your organization. I typically explore the 'Organization-in-the-mind' by asking them to make a drawing or to select an image out of a set of pictures presented. The typical questions asked are: Which picture best represents your organization today? Which picture best represents the desired organization?

Facts and figures are combined with associations about the current and future organization

For example, the picture below was selected as a representation of the current as well as the desired organization. The associations made were related to the working atmosphere (such as fun, excitement, playfulness), pride (for example, something unique, beautiful), work (hard work, we do it together) and growth (rapid, there is something frightening about growth).

Image representing today's and the desired organization (METALOG emotion cards)

When I looked at the survey results and my notes from the interviews, I felt a bit overwhelmed by the extent of the information and insights discovered. I decided to take some distance and to let it digest for a week. After this period of digestion, I started creating the report with my reflections, findings and recommendations.

Reflect before you act

As a next step, I shared the results with the CEO, COO and CHRO and we discussed the findings in depth. I wanted to take time with them to reflect on the findings before jumping to conclusions and actions. After sending them the report and as preparation for the face-to-face discussion, I asked them to reflect on the following questions: What comes to mind when you read the report (feelings, thoughts)? Do you find yourself in the main findings of the analysis? What are your personal 'take-aways'? What is your number one priority for increasing the efficiency of your organization? What do you hope will happen? What do you fear will happen? What will you personally do as the next step?

During the discussion, we also took the time to discuss findings at a more granular level for the different departments in the organization, while respecting the confidentiality thresholds defined.

The high response rate on the survey and openness during interviews showed high commitment and close involvement of most employees

A first interesting general finding was the high level of participation in the survey (93%). Also, the conversations during the one-on-one interviews were very open and many suggestions were made to make the organization a more efficient and better place to work. This is an important result in itself and reflects the commitment and close involvement of employees. Another hypothesis might be that it reflects the fact that people were not often invited to share their thoughts, concerns and frustrations. Moreover, the good intentions and drive to become better are deeply ingrained in the DNA of the organization and were clearly felt during the analysis phase of the project. This was a good starting position for implementing the transition to become future-proof.

In terms of general organizational strengths, I discovered that the organization is a fun place to work, has a unique atmosphere, and a common passion and drive. There is room for creativity and autonomy, and leaders have deep expertise and are accessible and involved. The structural and behavioural areas of improvement were related to decision making, meeting structure, involving colleagues, communication and flow of information, collaboration between teams, personal growth, trust and vulnerability, and pointing to one another's unproductive behaviour. I discovered that apart from the structural solutions to be taken to increase efficiency, critical shifts in mindset and behaviour had to be taken in seven areas: communication, involvement of the right people, (respecting) deadlines, agreements, decision making, dealing with unproductive behaviour and dealing with conflicts.

As a next step, we organized a second town hall session to present the results to all employees and to have first reflections and discussions. During this session we also presented the next steps (actions), which were grouped around four pillars: (1) clarifying and communicating the mission, vision, strategy, planning and objectives, (2) transition to a more efficiently structured organization (3) embedding the desired culture and behaviour and (4) further development of the HR function with a focus on softer HR elements. Employees were also invited to participate to create and execute the plans for these different areas. As an example, we created a core culture team to work on embedding the desired culture and behaviours, which was an important focus area to make the organization future-proof.

Practical mental tools helped employees to learn to self-reflect and learn to change their behaviour

For pillar two, a new organizational model, meeting structure, communication flow and decision-making framework was designed and introduced. For pillar four, a new HR manager was hired to focus on engagement, culture, on-boarding and employee experience, feedback and coaching, individual and team development, leadership development, well-being, and such. For pillar three, we conducted three-hour culture sessions for all employees (in groups of 15) as a first step in creating awareness about the conditions for behaviour change, to clarify and prioritize the desired behaviours and to learn (self-reflection) to apply two practical, mental tools that would support their shift in behaviour. Within the core team, we also developed and implemented a detailed approach and plan to further embed the desired culture.

Step by step, I started to see changes in awareness leading to changes in critical behaviours within the organization. 'I involve everyone who is needed in the process and consult the right people for input at the right time' was the first company-wide behaviour we started to embed in the organization. The impact of this single shift in behaviour on efficiency and motivation was huge. 'I respect deadlines and communicate honestly and clearly if deadlines are not met for some reason' was the second critical shift to be made. An important step to become future-proof was taken.

Three HUMAN-centred tactics

In the section below I want to share three human-centred tactics that I find to be highly impactful in building future-proof organizations:

1. Start with purpose, future success, the work to be done and the context around it.
2. Explore and grasp the full organizational potential by focusing on structural, motivational, and behavioural elements.
3. Minimize structures while focusing on empowered networks, critical behaviours, trust and fun.

On the following pages I elaborate on each of the three human-centred tactics in more detail.

Start with purpose, future success, the work to be done and the context around it

In many of the organizations I work with, when you ask leaders why their organizations do what they do – the purpose for their existence (also called the mission) or the future direction, and what it looks like when they succeed (the so-called 'vision') – they generally start by saying it is clear. But if you start asking for details, we often discover together that is not clear at all, or discover the misalignment about it among the leadership team.

⋮ *Imagine what future success looks like*

An important starting point for any initiative to prepare the organization for the future (reshape, optimize, (re)design) is to have a view about the future direction. A workshop format I often apply starts with visualizing what is in the mind when you think about the organization (step 1). In preparation for the workshop, I ask the participants to bring along a picture that represents the organization today. During the workshop, every participant sticks their picture on the wall and briefly explains why he/she chose this picture. At the end of the presentations, we have created an interesting view of the common associations related to the (perceived) organization today (the organization-in-the-mind).

For a Spanish company that is part of an international corporation, we started to design the future organization starting from the future success, the future work to be done and the context around it. In the example on the next page, the common associations made about the organization today were islands, stress, rat race, gratitude, talent and passion, unlocked energy and potential, and opportunities.

Example of the wall of pictures representing the organization today

As a next step during the workshop (step 2), we ask the participants to write down the three most significant trends that are happening today or that will be happening in the next five years, and will impact the organization. After the discussion, we have created a common view about the trends that will impact the company, and that create threats and opportunities.

The next step (3) is to create a first draft or to refine the mission statement, their purpose. The five questions asked in creating this statement are:

1. When you think of your organization, what makes you proud?
2. Why does your organization exist?
3. What is missing when your organization does not exist?
4. What does it look like when your organization is doing its best work/its utmost?
5. How does your organization make a difference for key stakeholders?

The answers of these discussions lead to the creation of the mission statement, which is built up by the three building blocks shown in the figure opposite.

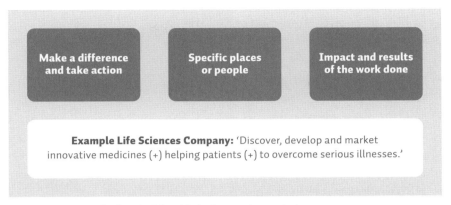

| Make a difference and take action | Specific places or people | Impact and results of the work done |

Example Life Sciences Company: 'Discover, develop and market innovative medicines (+) helping patients (+) to overcome serious illnesses.'

The three building blocks for creating a mission statement

To develop the vision (step 4), we often work in small groups as a first step. Each group is asked to make a drawing of the future organization. The drawing should represent the future ambitions and successes. As a second step, the groups are asked to write down the words associated with the drawing. Afterwards, each group presents the drawing, story, words to the whole team, which leads to a first draft of the mission statement of the company. The workshop is closed by creating the space for final reflections and the first discussion on the next steps to be taken.

Define what people (will) do and the context around it

Finding out what is really happening in the organization is an important initial step in any organization-related initiative. This sounds basic, but I see this confusion all the time. In order to analyze the work, I collect data about their key tasks, time spent, supporting tools used and meeting participation.

To get an understanding of the context of the work, I ask questions related to their goals, resources, constraints, key interactions, challenges, pride, frustrations and motivators. Keep in mind that behaviours are rational solutions in a particular context.

Examples of contextual questions asked are:

- What are you proud of?
- What are the key challenges in your role?
- What are you trying to achieve?
- How is success measured?
- What are the resources you use to achieve these goals (time, power, information, colleagues, etc.)?
- What hinders you in achieving these goals?
- With whom do you interact most?
- What frustrates you in your role?
- What motivates you in your role?

In the era of digitalization, it is critical to integrate perspectives related to the future of human work. In a recent *Harvard Business Review* article, Joseph Pistrui from IE Business School argues that the future of human work is imagination, creativity and strategy. This is important to keep in mind when designing the future organization.

TACTIC 2
Explore and grasp the full organizational potential by focusing on structural, motivational, and behavioural elements

Most organizational optimization projects start with a survey (quantitative method) combined with a selection of one-on-one interviews (qualitative method) with a representative sample of the organization. As in the story told above, it makes sense to invest in exploring the broad organizational scene and to focus on structural, motivational and behavioural dimensions.

Spotting the real challenges, strengths, and potential of the future organization

The survey and interviews give insights about the organizational strengths and points of improvement. Depending on the context of the project, I select a number of dimensions to be included in the spectrum to be analyzed:

☐ Factual overview of the work (key tasks, workload, etcetera) and context;
☐ Employee engagement, loyalty, pride, fun at work, well-being, energy drivers, stress drivers and coping mechanisms;
☐ Organizational effectiveness and efficiency;
☐ Psychological safety, level of trust among employees;
☐ Collaboration between the different teams and interpersonal dynamics;
☐ Perceived and desired values, culture and behaviours;
☐ Effectiveness of leadership.

A highly inspiring, fun workplace can significantly boost your performance and business bottom line

Daniel Cable, a professor at the London Business School, argues that the real war for talent is not hiring new employees from competitors but unleashing dormant enthusiasm in the existing workforce. How do you create an organization that people are proud to be part of, a working environment that is boosting human energy and business performance? Research shows that creating a highly inspiring, fun workplace can significantly boost your performance and business bottom line.

In general, employees were highly motivated and loyal

In the story told above, the first question was: How do we create a workplace where employees continue to feel good and happy? We found out that, in general, employees were highly motivated (Engagement Index is high). The presence of basic needs scores highly, as do individual and teamwork related needs. In terms of growth (how can I grow?), there was the most potential to increase engagement.

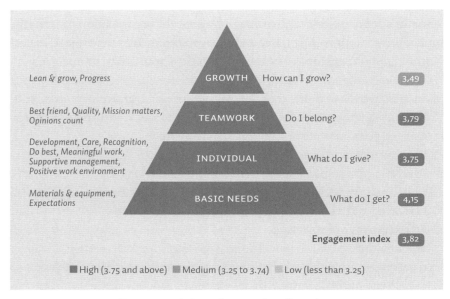

Engagement Index and score on key dimensions
(Source: The Q12 Employee Engagement model by Gallup)

I also measured the Employee Net Promoter Score (e-NPS) of the organization, a metric used to assess employee loyalty. The e-NPS is the percentage of unhappy employees subtracted from happy employees, as determined by their answer to the question 'On a scale of 0 to 10, how likely would you be to recommend this organization to a friend or colleague as a place to work?' The e-NPS was +20%, which is a good score.

The second question was: How do you increase the efficiency and effectiveness of the organization? Examples of strengths, and elements to keep that they brought up were: the pleasant working environment, unique atmosphere, the brand, space for creativity and innovation, flexibility with regard to the organization of own work, passion in what we do, the flat organizational structure and the responsibility taken by employees.

Examples of elements to change, to do differently were: not revisiting decisions taken, keeping to agreements made, working more often on a project basis, more effective consultation of colleagues, clearer and more logical roles and responsibilities, better flow of clear communication, making the vision and objectives more explicit, procrastination, feedback and evaluations, proactive learning and development.

Can we take risks in this organization without feeling insecure or embarrassed?

Is this a psychologically safe organization? We found out that the score was rather low, which meant that employees partially lack necessary levels of openness and vulnerability about individual strengths, weaknesses, mistakes and needs for help.

Psychological safety is defined as 'a belief that one will not be punished or humiliated for speaking up with ideas, questions, concerns, or mistakes'. If you do not feel safe in a group, you are likely to keep ideas to yourself and avoid speaking up, even about risks. Furthermore, if mistakes are held against you, you then look to avoid making mistakes and so stop taking risks, rather than making the most of your talents. Research shows that psychological safety is the gateway to success. This insight is the result of almost 30 years of research by Edmondson, which was supported and reinforced by an extensive two-year research programme by Google (Project Aristotle) among 15,000 employees.

See below some examples of measures to evaluate psychological safety:

- ☐ When someone makes a mistake in my organization, it is never held against him or her.
- ☐ In my organization, it is easy to discuss difficult issues and problems.
- ☐ In my organization, people are rarely rejected for being different.
- ☐ It is completely safe to take a risk in my organization.
- ☐ It is easy to ask other members of my organization for help.
- ☐ Members of my organization value and respect each other's contributions.

(Source: Amy C. Edmondson, The Fearless Organization Scan)

Based on the individual interviews, I gained the impression that, in general, employees have good intentions regarding working with other teams. There may be some interpersonal dynamics between (some) teams that make collaboration more difficult and create inefficiencies and frustrations.

These interpersonal dynamics in the collaboration led to a loss of efficiency (time and energy, reduced productivity) as well as a reduction in morale and motivation. Teams are thereby encouraged to 'off-tasks'; this means that team members can put a lot of effort, energy and time into dealing with these negative emotions and frustrations instead of concentrating on the organization's primary (business) task.

We discussed potential hypotheses and explanations for this. The survival dilemma might play an important role. The survival of any system – whether individual or group – depends on the interactions with its environment. This creates the dilemma: How can I maintain a sense of identity and continuity as a person (leading to preservation and isolation), and at the same time contribute to, and receive from others (leading to connection and integration)? I also assumed that the need for recognition (from leadership, from colleagues) unconsciously activates several defence mechanisms such as: gossiping about each other, painting each other black (discrediting each other), the urge to compare and distinguish oneself, and so on.

*Create awareness about interpersonal dynamics that promote or
hinder collaboration and its impact*

We also discussed tactics to improve collaboration (interpersonal dynamics) between teams. The first step is to become aware of the interpersonal dynamics that promote or hinder collaboration and to understand their impact. A reality check of the assumptions made about each other, as well as increasing trust between team members and developing more empathy (putting themselves in the other team's shoes) are subsequent ways of improving cooperation. Explicit recognition of teams, and a clear common vision are other solutions we implemented.

I assumed that there was also a series of assumptions and misunderstandings about one another (which were insufficiently checked against reality) that confirm and reinforce this behaviour. I also assumed that prejudices play a role: For example, the Horn effect describes how an opinion on negative aspects influences how other aspects are assessed. Confirmation bias is the tendency to search for or to interpret information that confirms existing beliefs.

Making shifts in critical behaviours

We discovered that apart from the structural solutions to be taken to increase efficiency, critical shifts in mindset and behaviour had to be taken in the following seven areas: communication, involvement of the right people, (respecting) deadlines, agreements, decision making, dealing with unproductive behaviour and dealing with conflicts. Some examples of (desired) behaviours to be changed were:

- I involve everyone who is needed in the process and consult the right people for input at the right time.
- I communicate deadlines, status updates and project expectations to involved colleagues.
- I communicate decisions made to colleagues who are impacted by this.
- I don't put off discussing problems and conflicts.
- I keep agreements made.
- If no clear decision has been made, I ask for clarification.
- I speak directly and constructively to colleagues if things don't go as they should.

Four action areas were defined to ensure that structural and behavioural improvements were implemented

As a next step, we organized a second town hall session to present the results and had a first discussion. During this session, we also presented the next steps (actions), which were grouped around four pillars: (1) clarifying and communicating the mission, vision, strategy, planning and objectives (2) transitioning to a more efficiently structured organization (3) embedding the desired culture and behaviour and (4) further developing the HR function with a focus on softer HR elements. Employees were also invited to participate in creating and executing the plans for these different areas.

How adaptable is your organization?

According to Deloitte, a new breed of successful organizations, called 'adaptive organizations' is emerging. These are shifting away from command-and-control cultures towards management practices that are unencumbered by excess bureaucracy, and that harness diverse crowds of people who are engaged, energized and focused on surprising and delighting customers, and who pursue both personal and business goals with purpose. They embrace change and rapidly morph to respond to shifting customer, environmental and market needs.

> *Adaptable organizations organize their capabilities away from deep hierarchy and silos towards a network of multidisciplinary teams*

The Adaptable Organization is a fundamental shift in operating and management philosophy that enables organizations to operate with a start-up mindset and drive modern people practices that enable enterprise agility through empowered networks of teams.

Is your organization ready to embrace adaptability? Consider the following questions as your initial assessment:

√ Do your workers, peripheral talent, and stakeholders truly see a shared purpose that unites them?

√ Does information from your customers and environment flow in seamlessly to inform decisions?

√ Have you minimized bureaucracy and hand-offs between teams?

√ Are you able to 'spin up' and 'spin down' teams rapidly when needed, with a clear mandate?

√ Do your teams operate based on trust, bringing diverse perspectives to the table, and perform well?

√ Are your people comfortable experimenting and learning from mistakes, knowing you will reward them for learning?

√ Do you know your leaders at every level?

✓ Do you know if your leaders have the capabilities needed for tomorrow's challenges?

✓ Do your talent programmes address talent beyond the traditional worker, such as contingent workers?

✓ Can you support your people in building their skills and capabilities across a range of experiences, or are they encouraged to continually move up?

Quick assessment to evaluate the adaptability of your organization (Source: Deloitte)

TACTIC 3
Minimize structures while focusing on empowered networks, critical behaviours, trust and fun

Organizations today are largely structured in the same way they have been for a century. I find that today's management systems, structures and talent strategies tend to be outdated and are designed for an era when size and enduring stability defined competitive advantage.

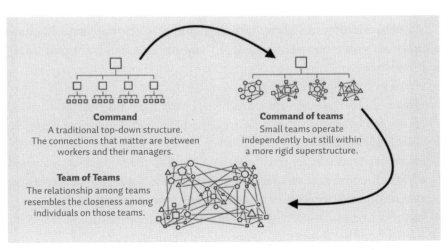

The future of organizations (Source: Team of Teams: New rules of engagement for a complex world Team of Teams by McChrystal)

I strongly believe in McChrystal's 'Team of Teams' in which organizations operate as empowered networks, coordinated through culture, information systems, and talent mobility. This new mode of organization – a 'network of teams' – is now sweeping public and private organizations in all sectors around the world.

People must have the system perspective and context before they're empowered with authority.

McChrystal argues that in order for teams to think and act as one, they need to build shared consciousness, which in turn requires two things: (1) systemic understanding such that people can see the big picture and understand how their work is interdependent; and (2) strong lateral connectivity between teams, through personal relationships between individual team members. Empowered execution is a second important element. For a Team of Teams to be born, leaders must be willing to let go and to share power. This goes beyond delegation: leaders must deliberately encourage and nurture decision-making skills at all levels. It's also critical that a foundation of shared consciousness is already in place – otherwise, it'll be disastrous to simply remove constraints and allow people to do whatever they want.

An empowered network of teams

These networks of teams are typically built on several principles to facilitate a high degree of empowerment, strong communication, and rapid information flow:

- Move people into customer-, product-, or market- and mission-focused teams, led by team leaders who are experts in their domain (not 'professional managers').
- Empower teams to set their own goals and make their own decisions within the context of an overarching strategy or business plan, reversing the traditional structure of goal and performance management.
- Introduce team-based tools to share integrated information and identify connections between team activities and desired results.

- Teach and encourage people to work across teams, using open office spaces that promote collaboration and job rotation to give teams a common understanding of one another.
- Shift senior leaders into roles focused on planning, strategy, vision, culture, and cross-team communication.
- Optimize performance management around 'team performance' rather than focusing solely on individual performance and designating individuals as leaders simply by virtue of their title or role. Reward people for project results, collaboration, and helping others.

Earlier, I talked about the Spanish company that is part of an international corporation. In this case, we designed the future organization by starting from future success, the future work to be done and its context. For the relevant organizational dimensions, we defined the future state: organizational model, roles, coordination and decisions, talent and capabilities, culture/behaviours, leadership, processes and tools, external orientation, and innovation and learning. Afterwards, the transition to the new organization focused on a number of action areas: role allocation taking into account the succession needs of key people in the organization, building psychological safety, implementing the new meeting structure and decision-making framework, leadership development and the shift towards new critical behaviours.

Embedding a collaborative mindset and empathy was essential for building a nimble, flexible, team-centred organizational structure

I like to take you back to the story I told about before (Speed, Gears and Brakes). To realize the shift in critical behaviours, as a first step, we conducted three-hour culture sessions for all employees (in groups of 15) to create awareness about the conditions for a change in behaviour, to clarify and prioritize the desired behaviours and to learn (self-reflection) to apply two practical, mental tools that would support their change in behaviour.

An example of a mental tool to embed a collaborative mindset and empathy is the 'principle of charity'. It offers a simple methodological prescription for fighting our natural tendency to treat our own interpretations as facts. See chapter 3.

How to make work more fun

The Corporate Rebels is a global movement with the mission to make work more fun. I met them in 2017 and partnered with them on some projects. They have travelled around the world and visited over 150 workplace pioneers, entrepreneurs, academics, organizations, and leaders – each of whom has succeeded by working in radically different ways. Based on this, they uncovered and identified eight habits that clearly distinguish the truly progressive organizations from the others:

1. From profit to purpose & values
2. From hierarchical pyramids to networks of teams
3. From directive to supportive leadership
4. From plan & predict to experiment & adapt
5. From rules & control to freedom & trust
6. From centralized authority to distributed decision making
7. From secrecy to radical transparency
8. From job descriptions to talents & mastery

The eight habits that clearly distinguish truly progressive organizations from the others

Check it out: How do you measure against eight characteristics of highly inspiring workplaces?

		1	2	3	4	5	
Purpose & Values	Visions and values are not guiding within the organization	CURRENT					Visions and values are applied daily and are guiding
		DESIRED					
Networks of Teams	Fully hierarchical organization	CURRENT					Organization consisting of networks of teams
		DESIRED					
Supportive Leadership	No servant/ supportive leadership	CURRENT					Full servant/ supportive leadership
		DESIRED					
Experiment & Adapt	Prediction and planning-based approach	CURRENT					Experimentation and agile working approach
		DESIRED					
Freedom & Trust	Fully controlled	CURRENT					Full freedom & Trust
		DESIRED					
Distributed Decision Making	Centralized top-down decision-making process	CURRENT					Bottom-up decision-making process
		DESIRED					
Radical Transparency	Full secrecy	CURRENT					Full disclosure of information
		DESIRED					
Talents & Mastery	Task allocated based on job description	CURRENT					Everyone does what they do best without fixed job description
		DESIRED					

Quick scan on the eight trends of highly inspiring workplaces
(Source: The Corporate Rebels)

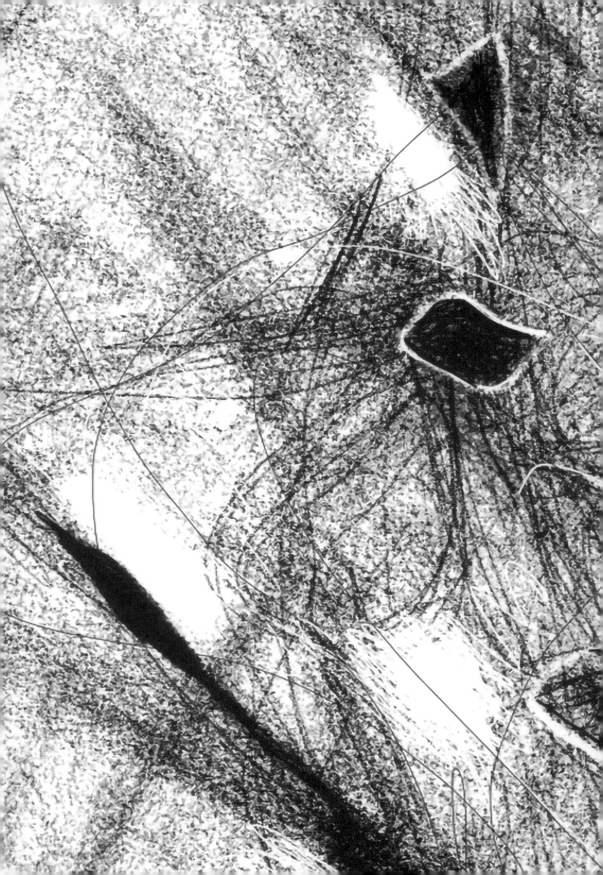

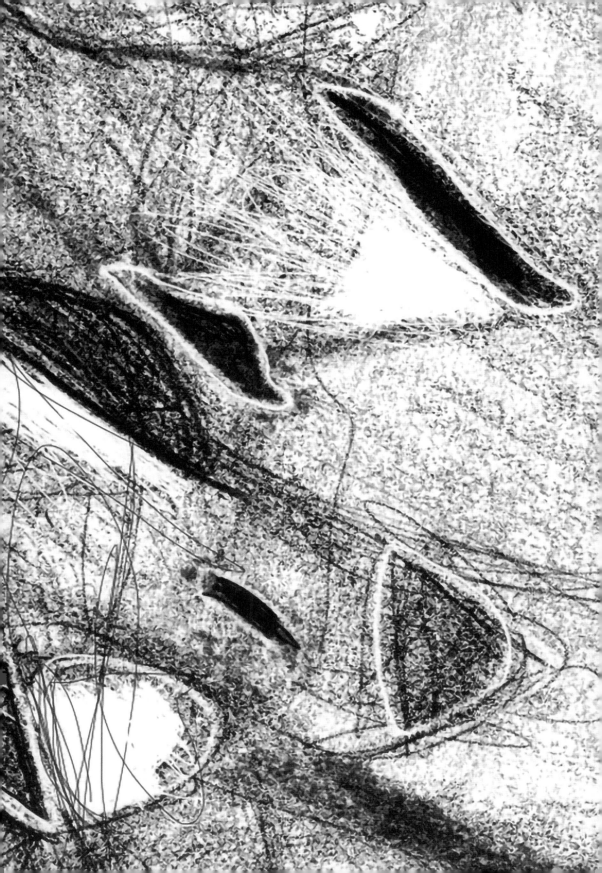

← PREVIOUS PAGES

Peter's narrative

Fluid energized Network System

A visionary, artistic drawing of energized networks to inspire associates to release their imagination and create fluid systems and communication in the organization. Analysis and observation are strengthened by going away to their opposites, intuition, and imagination.

Summarizing the main points

Building a future-proof organization with efficiency, values, trust and fun at its heart

- **How future work is organized** within organizations and the broader eco-systems is a significant accelerator in the performance of organizations. It significantly impacts future value creation, staying relevant and survival.

- **Inefficiency, rigidity, complexity, high costs, conflicts, politics, disengagement, people don't feel well, lack of pride and fun** are frustrations and concerns I often hear when I talk to leaders about their organization.

- Leaders ask themselves: **Will I/we be able to deal effectively with the rapidly changing challenges** or, even more fundamentally, will I/we stay relevant and survive?

- **Three less conventional tactics** that have proven to be highly impactful in building future-proof organizations:

  1. Start with purpose, future success, the work to be done and the context around it
  2. Explore and grasp the full organizational potential by focusing on structural, motivational, and behavioural elements.
  3. Minimize structures while focusing on empowered networks, critical behaviours, trust and fun.

- It pays off to **explore the potential of organizations in terms of structural organizational elements combined with motivational and behavioural elements.** The latter is often underexposed in organizational initiatives and leads to solutions that do not solve the real issue(s).

- **A new mode of organization** – 'Team of Teams' – is now sweeping organizations around the world. These networks of teams operate as empowered networks, coordinated through culture, information systems, and talent mobility.

- **Building empowered networks, installing psychological safety (empathy) and facilitating critical shifts in behaviours** were essential areas of investment in almost any organizational initiatives I have consulted on.

▶ How to get started

▶ **How future-proof is your organization today** on a scale of 0 to 10? Please describe the concerns, first thoughts you have today.

Think of inefficiency, rigidity, complexity, high costs, conflicts, politics, disengagement, well-being issues, lack of pride or fun.

TACTIC 1
Start with purpose, future success, the work to be done and the context around it

▶ **Imagine future success and refine/define the vision of your organization.**

Step 1: Set up a meeting with a group of colleagues and make a drawing (together) that represents your organization's future state of ambitions and success.

Step 2: As a second step, write down the words associated with these drawings.

Step 3: Based on the drawings and associations, complete the following sentence: In five years, we want to be ...

Step 4: You have your vision statement!

Some tips:
- The declaration begins with an intention such as 'We want to be'.
- Try to summarize your vision using a powerful phrase.
- The vision statement is intended to inspire, activate, motivate and stimulate your creativity.

TACTIC 2

Explore and grasp the full organizational potential by focusing on structural, motivational, and behavioural elements

▶ **Explore the 'Organization-in-the-mind'**

- Look for a picture (on the internet) that represents your organization today and ask a selection of colleagues (representative of your organization) to do the same.
- Set up a meeting with your group of colleagues and stick your and your colleagues' pictures on the wall and briefly explain why this picture has been chosen.
- By the end of the presentations, you will have created a view of the common associations related to your organization today.
- What did you discover?

▶ **Evaluate how you score on the different dimensions of high-performing organizations.**

What are the organizational **strengths** you have to realize this vision?

Take the different dimensions of a high-performing organization shown on the next page as reference for reflection.

Mission / Vision / Strategy

Clear and compelling vision, direction where your organization is heading and how to get there (strategy)

Organization model

Overall picture on how the work to be executed is grouped and key interactions between the groups.

Roles & accountabilities

Individuals understand what is expected of them, have enough authority and feel accountable for delivering results.

Coordination & decisions

Clear decision-making process at strategic and operational level. Exchange of relevant information between teams, throughout the organization.

Leadership

Effective leadership style to inspire people, shape their actions and drive performance.

Skilled and engaged talent

Required skills and capabilities are in place to execute the work. Loyal and enthusiastic employees performing at their very best.

Culture / behaviours

Clear, consistent set of values and working norms that foster effective workplace behaviours.

Supporting processes & tools

Process and tools supporting the work to be done.

External orientation

Engage with important stakeholders to more effectively create and deliver value (now and in the future)

Innovation & Learning

Encourage and harness new ideas from radical innovation to incremental improvement.

The 10 building blocks of high-performing organizations

- What are the organizational **weaknesses** you have today to realize this vision? See above as reference for reflection.

► **Measure the engagement level.**

How would you score the statements below on a scale of 1 (Strongly Disagree) to 5 (Strongly Agree)? Use below statements as a reference for reflection.

Statement	Hierarchy	Score
I am satisfied with my organization as a place to work	Engagement	
I know what is expected of me at work	Basic needs	
I have the materials and equipment I need to do my work right	Basic needs	
At work, I have the opportunity to do what I do best every day	Individual	
In the last seven days, I have received recognition or praise for doing good work	Individual	
My supervisor or someone at work seems to care about me as a person	Individual	
There is someone at work who encourages my development	Individual	
At work, my opinions seem to count	Teamwork	
The mission or purpose of my organization makes me feel my job is important	Teamwork	
My associates are committed to doing quality work	Teamwork	
I have a best friend at work	Teamwork	
In the last six months, someone at work has talked to me about my progress	Grow	
This last year, I have had opportunities at work to learn and grow	Grow	

(Source: Gallup Engagement Questionnaire)

What are your areas (basic needs, individual, teamwork, growth) where you score strongest and weakest in terms of engagement?

TACTIC 3
Minimize structures while focusing on empowered networks, critical behaviours and psychological safety

▶ **Brainstorm about the desired behaviours in your organization; the ones that ensure the vision of your organization will be achieved.**

Tip: Think about specific behaviours related to (1) interactions with others (2) use of time (3) decision making.

▶ **Please select the one change in behaviour that will have the biggest impact.**

For this selected behaviour, please answer the three questions below:

· What do you want to SEE? And, what don't you want to SEE ?
· What do you want people to SAY? And, what don't you want people to SAY ?
· What do you want people to THINK? And, what don't you want people to THINK?

▶ Increase the level of trust, psychological safety.

There will be more trust within the organization if employees:

☐ Let go of grudges
☐ Admit their mistakes
☐ Reduce the amount of gossiping
☐ Spend more time together
☐ Get to know each other on a personal level
☐ Are more forthright with information
☐ Readily apologize
☐ Share professional failures and successes
☐ Give credit where credit is due
☐ Understand each other's working style

▶ **Take a step back and define the key insights you discovered about your organization and how future-proof you are.** Please describe.

▶ **Build your improvement plan: What are the structural and behavioural actions you suggest taking?**

Where would you invest in order to make your organization more future-proof (and realize the vision)?

☐ The mission, vision or strategy to reach the vision
☐ The way we interact, coordinate, communicate, exchange information
☐ Roles, accountabilities, authority
☐ Decision making at strategic or operational level
☐ Required skills and capabilities
☐ Engagement, enthusiasm, or loyalty of employees
☐ Values, mindset, working norms and behaviours
☐ Leadership style or effectiveness to inspire people, shape their actions and drive performance
☐ Trust within the organization
☐ Supporting processes and tools
☐ Stakeholder management or (external) orientation
☐ Learning and innovation

▶ **What did you learn? What are you going to do next?**

....
....
....
....
....

Good luck!

'Trust men, and they will be true to you; treat them greatly and they will show themselves great.'

– Ralph Waldo Emerson

Chapter 5: **Key references and interesting reads**

Armstrong, D. (2010. *Organization in the Mind: Psychoanalysis, Group Relations, and Organizational Consultancy, Occasional Papers 1989-2003.* London: Karnac.

Barrett, R. (2017). *The values-driven organization: Cultural health and employee well-being as a pathway to sustainable performance.* New York, NY: Routledge.

Bridges, W., & Mitchel, S. (2000). Leading Transition: A New Model for Change. *Leader to Leader*, Nr. 16.

Collins, J. C. (2009). Good to great: *Why some companies make the leap ... and others don't.* New York, NY: Collins.

Collins, J. C., & Porras, J. I. (1997). *Built to last: Successful habits of visionary companies.* New York: Harper Business.

Complicatedness Survey. Retrieved December 11, 2020, from https://www.bcg.com/capabilities/smart-simplicity/complicatedness-survey

Cooper, A., & Dartington, T. (2004). The vanishing organization: Organizational containment in a networked world. In C. Huffington, D. Armstrong, W. Halton, L. Hoyle, & J. Pooley (Eds.). Working below the surface. *The emotional life of contemporary organizations* (pp. 127–150). London: Karnac.

Csíkszentmihályi, M. (1997). *Finding flow: The psychology of engagement with everyday life.* New York, US: Basic Books.

Deloitte (2019). Global Human Capital Trends: Organizational performance: It's a team sport.

Deloitte (2017). Insights article: Organizational design: The rise of teams.

Edmondson, A. C. (2019). *The fearless organization: Creating psychological safety in the workplace for learning, innovation, and growth.* Hoboken, N.J.: John Wiley & Sons.

Gladwell, M. (2015). *The tipping point: How little things can make a big difference.* London: Abacus.

Hastings, R., & Meyer, E. (2020). *No rules rules: Netflix and the culture of reinvention.* New York: Penguin Press.

Heifetz, R., Grashow, A., & Linsky, M. (2009). *The Practice of Adaptive Leadership: Tools and Tactics for Changing Your Organization and the World.* Boston, Massachusetts: Harvard Business School Publishing.

Hirschhorn, L. (1997). *Reworking authority. Leading and following in the post-modern organization.* Cambridge, MA: The MIT Press.

Hirschhorn, L., & Gilmore, T. (1992). The New Boundaries of the 'Boundaryless' Company. *Harvard Business Review, 70*(3), 104-115.

Huffington, C., Armstrong, D., Halton, W., Hoyle, L., & Pooley, J. (Eds.). (2004). *Working below the surface. The emotional life of contemporary organizations.* London: Karnac.

Keller, S. (2011). *Beyond performance: How great organizations build ultimate competitive advantage.* Hoboken, N.J.: Wiley.

Laloux, F. (2014). *Reinventing organizations: A guide to creating organizations inspired by the next stage of human consciousness.* Brussels: Nelson Parker.

Leberecht, T. (2015). *Business Romantic: Fall back in love with your work and your life.* Place of publication not identified: Piatkus Books.

Long, S. (2013). *Socioanalytic Methods: Discovering the Hidden in Organisations and Social Systems.* London: Karnac.

McChrystal, S. A., Collins, T., Silverman, D., & Fussell, C. (2015). *Team of Teams: New rules of engagement for a complex world.* NY, NY: Portfolio/Penguin.

Morieux, Y., & Tollman, P. (2014). *Six simple rules: how to manage complexity without getting complicated.* Boston, MA: Harvard Business Review Press.

Nayar, V. (2010). *Employees first, customers second: Turning conventional management upside down.* Boston, MA: Harvard Business Press.

Palmer, B., & Reed, B. (1971). An introduction to Organizational Behaviour. Retrieved from http://www.grubbinstitute.org.uk

Taylor, K. (2017). Deloitte article: At a tipping point? Workplace mental health and wellbeing.

Thaler, R. H., & Sunstein, C. R. (2008). *Nudge: Improving decisions using the architecture of choice.* New Haven, CT: Yale University Press.

The 8 habits of the world's most progressive workplaces. (n.d.). Retrieved August 06, 2020, from https://www.maize.io/en/content/the-8-habits-of-world-s-most-progressive-workplaces

The Adaptable Organization. (n.d.). Retrieved August 06, 2020, from https://www2.deloitte.com/global/en/pages/human-capital/articles/the-adaptable-organization.html

Weiss, L. (2019). *How we work: Live your purpose, reclaim your sanity, and embrace the daily grind.* New York, NY: Harper Wave, an imprint of HarperCollins.

WHO, 2014. Mental health: a state of well-being, WHO, 2014. See also: http://www.who.int/features/factfiles/mental_health/en/

Bringing it all together

'We don't see things as they are,
we see them as we are.'

– Anaïs Nin

A systems psychodynamic approach

In this chapter, I intend to bring the five previous chapters together from a more methodological perspective. This will sum up how to humanize your efforts to realize your strategy. The approach in dealing with the challenges described in chapters 1 to 5 is what I call a socio-technical approach; the approach combines a structural, technical perspective with a psychological perspective, focusing on human dynamics. In my experience, the structural, technical dimension is mostly well embedded in the basic logic of leaders in dealing with strategic challenges. The more human and psychological part is often missing in terms of perspective, approach, and solutions. Therefore, I emphasize the human-centrism of the approach in this book.

People are complex, unique, and paradoxical beings with rich and myriad motivational drivers and decision-making and interaction patterns (Manfred Kets de Vries)

The approach applied integrates the research-based concepts of systems psychodynamics. This approach focuses on the dynamics of human behaviour that are often the most difficult to understand. It acknowledges that people are complex, unique, and paradoxical beings with rich and myriad motivational drivers and decision-making and interaction patterns. Applying psychodynamic concepts in organizations contributes to our understanding of the vicissitudes of life and leadership. Manfred Kets de Vries argues that only in understanding ourselves and our drivers, and in turn turning our analytic gaze to deciphering the motivations and behaviours of others around us, can we truly understand the complexity of the system in which we live and work.

The psychodynamic approach provides another lens to the study of organizational dynamics beyond a purely rational, structural approach. Specifically, it addresses the undercurrents of organizational life through issues such as interpersonal communication, group processes, social defences, and organization-wide neurosis. Another strength is that the psychodynamic approach involves an in-depth and systemic investigation of a single person, group, event or community. It consists not only of an analysis of the self but also of the self in relation to others and to the context in which he or she exists.

Only through accepting and exploring the hidden undercurrents that affect human behaviour can we begin to understand organizational life in all its complexities

The Clinical Paradigm is the framework through which a psychodynamic lens to the study of behaviour in organizations is applied. The Clinical Paradigm consists of four basic premises.

First, it argues that there is a rationale behind every human act – a logical explanation – even for actions that seem irrational. This point of view stipulates that all behaviour has an explanation.

The second premise is that a great deal of mental life – feelings, fears, motives – lies outside of conscious awareness, but still affects conscious reality and even physical well-being. We all have blind spots. People are not always aware of what they are doing – much less why they are doing it.

The third premise states that nothing is more central to who a person is than the way he or she regulates and expresses emotions. Emotions colour experiences with positive and negative connotations, creating preference in the choices we make, and in the way we deal with the world.

The fourth premise underlying the clinical paradigm is that human development is an inter- and intrapersonal process; we are all products of our past experiences, and those experiences, including the developmental experiences provided by our early caregivers, continue to influence us throughout life.

Systems psychodynamic tools provide a way to look at the hidden dynamics and undercurrents of organizational behaviour to decipher the motives for why people behave the way they do

Key concepts of systems psychodynamics have been interwoven in the approach as described in chapters 1 to 5. Examples of these concepts are: the Core Conflictual Relationship Theme (CCRT), the survival dilemma of individuals and groups, social defences, tipping points, associative thinking (based on drawings or pictures), the reflective and transitional space, working notes with hypotheses (I wonder if …), mental models, 'collaboration-in-the-mind', and so on.

The five-step approach to humanize your strategy

At a more conceptual and high level, each of the three human-centred tactics explained in chapters 1 to 5 fits into a five-step approach as visualized in the figure on the next page; this is the approach I developed and apply to humanize strategies and it significantly increases the success of realizing these.

The 5 critical steps are:

1. State (what you think is) the issue.
2. Explore and discover insights related to the challenges above (visible) and below (invisible) the surface.
3. Name the real issue and create an understanding as to why it happens and its impact on performance.
4. Implement structural and behavioural tactics to solve the real issue.
5. Reinforce and embed the change.

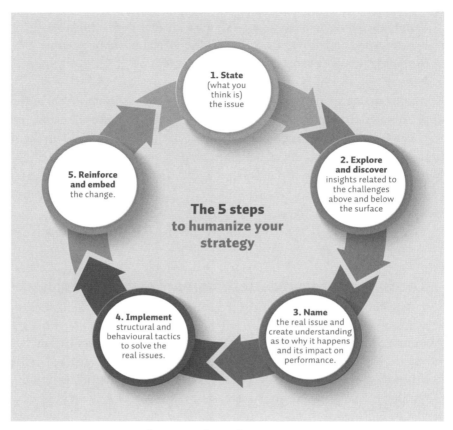

The 5 steps to humanize your strategy

Step 1: **State (what you think is) the issue.**

During this first step, the sponsor of the project makes explicit how he/she understands the challenge, issue or problem he/she is facing. Typically, several worrying signs have been observed, like a decrease in performance, an increase in turn-over rates, complacency, more conflict, a lack of decision making or planning or a failure to realize these, fear of failure, working in silos, etc. Quite often, when I meet them, they have already tried several (mostly technically focused) approaches to deal with the challenges and fix the problem, most of which did not bring the expected results.

Often, organizations have already tried several (technical) approaches to fix the problem

The issues that are often channelled are described in the different chapters of this book: Why is so much time, effort and energy of team members side-tracked by emotions, tensions, and conflicts? (Chapter 1). Why don't we get rid of the silos within my organization? (Chapter 2). Why don't people in my organization act and focus in accordance with our strategic objectives? (Chapter 3). Why don't the people in my organization engage with the vision I have already shared? (Chapter 4). Why is my organization not ready to deal effectively with rapidly changing challenges? (Chapter 5).

The severity of the issues I encounter varies from small issues to real crises like the story in chapter 1, where the leadership team was so dysfunctional that it blocked them from grasping any growth opportunities. Also, after some 'scratching the surface' (see step 2), the issues are quite often different in terms of severity or even scope from the problem that was stated initially. This is why I describe this first step as 'what you think is the challenge'.

'Scratching the surface'

At the start of a project, I typically have multiple discussions with the sponsor in order to build trust, contain anxiety and evaluate the readiness to deal with the challenge. I find it worth the investment to spend substantial time on this. Typically, the coaching on relevant areas with the sponsor starts as of step 1.

In my experience, a what I call 'sponsor readiness check' should be conducted before starting the project/initiative. Only if the sponsor answers YES to the three questions below, I believe it makes sense to start the initiative. If not, the chances of successful interventions will significantly decrease.

1. Are you serious about making your strategy a success?
2. Do you have the patience to keep asking 'why'?
3. Do you have the courage to take a less conventional approach?

Step 2: Explore and discover insights related to the challenges above and below the surface

In chapter 2, we discussed that the start of a collaboration can be conscious and rational, that the process is often influenced by hidden, emotional and unconscious motives and human dynamics. In this case, decoding the intrapersonal, interpersonal, intra-team or inter-team dynamics is the key objective of this second step.

The scope of the systemic approach depends on the challenge faced. For example, to make a team act as one team (chapter 1), the scope is on intra- and interpersonal dynamics.

Demystifying human dynamics

During this step, I often work with the metaphor of the iceberg. The iceberg is like the mind; the conscious mind is what we notice above the surface, while the unconscious mind, the largest and most powerful part, remains unseen below the surface. I am particularly interested in working 'below the surface' and drawing attention to underlying, mostly unconscious patterns of emotions, values, beliefs, thoughts, assumptions, priorities, fantasies, that drive engagement and behaviour (potential blind spots).

Exploring the underlying, mostly unconscious patterns of emotions, thoughts, and assumptions, that drive engagement and behaviour

In this step, research-based qualitative and quantitative methods are applied to discover what is really going on from a technical as well as a systems psychodynamic perspective with a focus on values, beliefs, emotions, and hidden underlying motivational forces that influence individual and collective behaviour.

Step 3: Name the real issue and create understanding as to why it happens and its impact on performance

In this step, the key focus is on consolidating the finding (technical as well as psychological), reporting back to the relevant stakeholders and discussing these findings with them. It is important to take time to reflect. I have experienced that jumping to conclusions or acting hastily is a potential pitfall.

> *I wonder if … happens, because of …*

An important discussion is about the hypotheses regarding the behaviours manifested; why they happen and their impact (I wonder if … happens, because of …). This is also the step during which we evaluate the strengths and potential for improvement. Understanding how much effort, energy and time is dedicated to managing emotions and frustrations (to deal with the issue) instead of dealing with the primary task of the organization is a perspective to gain during this step.

> *How much time, effort and energy is spent on dealing with emotions and frustrations (and not on the primary tasks of the organization)?*

As an example, the hidden human dynamics related to the 'survival dilemma' have a big impact on performance in many of the stories I told. As a reminder, the survival of any system – whether individual or group – depends on the interactions with its environment. This creates the dilemma: How can I maintain a sense of identity and continuity as a person (leading to preservation and isolation), and at the same time contribute to, and receive from others (leading to connection and integration)? I learned that this dilemma can be a big energy drain at individual, team, across teams and even organizational levels.

During this step, we aim to trigger, provoke and create tipping points for change. Remember that tipping points are 'Aha!' moments, sudden moments of insight that make everything click and result in changes, shifts in awareness, which lead to changes in behaviour.

Step 4: Implement structural and behavioural tactics to solve the real issue

Often interventions to build high-performing teams, improve collaboration across teams, develop leaders, shift cultures and build future-proof organizations do not tackle the root cause but simply fix its manifestations.

In this step, it is critical to identify the type of challenge you are dealing with: adaptive or technical. A technical challenge is defined as one that can be solved by the knowledge of experts, whereas the adaptive challenge requires new learning. When the problem definition, solution, and implementation is clear, Heifetz calls this technical change. Adaptive challenges are characterized by changes in people's priorities, beliefs, habits, and loyalties, and require learning during the process of problem definition and solution.

> *The biggest failure of leadership is to treat adaptive challenges like technical problems (Heifetz)*

It is key to name the real issues so we can start implementing the appropriate structural and behavioural tactics to deal with these. Examples of behavioural strategies that have been brought up are installing trust and psychological safety, creating shifts in mindset, and changing behaviours, etc. Using mental tools to facilitate changing behaviours is another practice we often apply and that pays off. The figure opposite explains the difference between technical problems and adaptive challenges as well as how to deal with them.

TECHNICAL PROBLEMS VERSUS ADAPTIVE CHALLENGES

Technical problems

1. Easy to identify
2. Often lend themselves to quick and easy (cut-and-dried) solutions
3. Often can be solved by an authority or expert
4. Require change in just one or a few places; often contained within organizational boundaries
5. People are generally receptive to technical solutions
6. Solutions can often be implemented quickly

Adaptive challenges

1. Difficult to identify (easy to deny)
2. Require changes in values, beliefs, roles, relationships & approaches to work
3. People with the problem do the work of solving it
4. Require change in numerous places; usually cross-organizational boundaries
5. People often resist even acknowledging adaptive challenges
6. 'Solutions' require experiments and new discoveries; they can take a long time to implement and cannot be implemented by edict

The difference between technical problems and adaptive challenges (Source: The Practice of Adaptive Leadership by Heifetz, Grashow & Linsky)

Distinguishing technical problems and adaptive challenges			
Kind of challenge	Problem definition	Solution	Locus of work
Technical	Clear	Clear	Authority
Technical and adaptive	Clear	Requires learning	Authority and stakeholders
Adaptive	Requires learning	Requires learning	Stakeholders

How to best deal with different types of challenges? (Source: The Practice of Adaptive Leadership by Heifetz, Grashow & Linsky)

Step 5: **Reinforce and embed the change**

I learned that the language used by the people involved in a change is an important indicator to evaluate the embedding of change. Deep listening is a great tool to evaluate the current status and to define additional actions to reinforce or further embed the changes you have in mind.

As explained in chapter 3, Bridges' three-phase model of transition is also relevant in this step in order to manage the emotional change effectively. The first phase of transition is to let go, followed by the neutral zone, an in-between state that is full of uncertainty and confusion. After this, behaving in a new way can begin.

The mental tool 'competing commitments' explained before helps to embed change in mindset and behaviours. As a reminder, in the book *The Real Reason People Won't Change*, Kegan and Lahey show how our individual beliefs along with the collective mindsets in organizations combine to create a natural but powerful immunity to change. They assert that change is extremely difficult, be it on the personal or the organizational level, due to hidden competing commitments, major assumptions and ingrained thought patterns that discourage individuals and teams from abandoning the status quo.

If a consultant or coach is facilitating this process, this final step also includes the handover of the initiative to the sponsor and 'letting go' of the initiative for the consultant/coach.

Critical roles to humanize your strategy

YOUR ROLE AS A LEADER

Needless to say, as a leader/sponsor you have a key role to play in initiatives to make teams act as ONE team, build organizations where people work together spontaneously across teams, make people act and focus in line with the strategy, inspire and create commitment to the strategy or to build future-proof organizations.

As described above, the 'sponsor readiness check' at the start of the project is key. Are you serious about making your strategy a success? Do you have the patience to keep asking 'why'? Do you have the courage to take a less conventional approach?

Leading change requires facing ambiguity, uncertainty, and tensions without falling into the position of judging others

As leader, you need to know that you are part of the system and have a critical role to play (and model) throughout the transition. Leading the transition requires leadership to be able to face ambiguity, uncertainty, and tensions without falling into the position of judging others. Leading these initiatives involves creating conditions for the different parties to come to a common problem definition and strategy, and tactics to deal with it.

As leader, you will be often dealing with an adaptive challenge (rather than a technical problem), which means that an adaptive leadership style is required to make it happen. The six principles of leading adaptive change as described by Heifetz are to (1) get on the balcony (create distance to see the big picture) (2) identify the adaptive challenge (3) regulate distress (not overwhelm but provide enough tension to maintain urgency, challenge unproductive norms, ask questions rather than give answers) (4) maintain disciplined attention (5) give work back to the people and (6) protect voices of leadership from below.

Lack of knowledge, risk aversion and anxiety to deal with emotions are reasons why human-centric approaches are not applied by leaders

The key challenges for leaders I encounter are to take time to reflect (not jump to conclusions), to be open and give time to let solutions emerge, to show vulnerability, and to be courageous enough to take a less conventional approach. Both lack of knowledge about how to deal with changes and the risk aversion of leaders play a role, but so too does anxiety about dealing with emotions (the fear of opening Pandora's box). This is a human, natural reaction and I often coach and support leaders on these challenges.

As a leader, you will often have gone through a (personal) transition requiring self-reflection, and showing (situational) vulnerability. As a role model, you have to be aware of what you do (sometimes unconscious), why you do it and its impact. Therefore, this type of initiative creates great opportunities for leadership development and growth.

THE ROLE OF THE CONSULTANT/COACH

Often, a consultant/coach is asked to facilitate the process to solve the issues we have talked about. Based on my experience, the reason for this is two-fold. A consultant/coach can bring deep technical expertise, but especially a systems psychodynamic lens, which is required to deal with the potential adaptive challenges faced. Secondly, it is essential in some cases to have someone involved from the outside, who is not part of the system.

A hybrid support model combining and alternating the roles of consultant and coach

As facilitator of the process, I often apply a hybrid support model combining and alternating the roles of consultant and coach. Sometimes during steps 1 to 5 it is valuable to give advice, be more directive and provide solutions (consultant); at other times it makes more sense to help the client find their own answers (coach). This combined approach makes sense because of the increase in complexity and knowledge required to solve the problem and the focus on learning through joint exploration.

I see my role as being the creator of a safe, reflective space, allowing the participants to engage in the exploration of insights at conscious and emotional, unconscious levels. My role is also to be the comforter and to – temporarily – contain the anxieties stirred up by the uncertainty and ambiguity of the process. I also see my role as being a creator of the right dose of tension (at the right level and right moment), and to trigger or provoke shifts in awareness and actions – tipping points.

I often have to tolerate the tension of not knowing and of not being in control. In my experience, it makes sense to allow time to digest and be open to what emerges. I often use myself as an instrument and use personal reflection and associations to come up with hypotheses on what might be really happening.

How you partner with your client defines the value you bring and the impact you have

My personal mission and the mission of the company I founded (B15) is to work with leaders to solve their most critical issues by including human-centred strategies that work in their unique context. The six values and behaviours we embody to support this mission are:

1. We are independent, trusted advisors with the courage to say what needs to be said.
2. We are active listeners and are curious to understand your unique context.
3. We are at ease with uncertainty and uncomfortable situations.
4. We really want to make it work and do not give up easily.
5. We care, and show respect, empathy, and compassion.
6. We go for excellence in all we do in a humble way.

I have experienced that the way you act as consultant/coach and how you partner with your client defines the value you bring, the difference you make and the impact you have.

'It is more important to know where you are going than to get there quickly. Do not mistake activity for achievement.'

– Mabel Newcomer

Chapter 6: **Key references and interesting reads**

Armstrong, D. (2010). *Organization in the Mind: Psychoanalysis, Group Relations, and Organizational Consultancy, Occasional Papers 1989-2003*. London: Karnac.

Bollas, C. (1987). *The shadow of the object: Psychoanalysis of the unthought known*. New York, NY: Columbia University Press.

Heifetz, R., Grashow, A., & Linsky, M. (2009). *The Practice of Adaptive Leadership: Tools and Tactics for Changing Your Organization and the World*. Boston, Massachusetts: Harvard Business School Publishing.

Gladwell, M. (2015). *The tipping point: How little things can make a big difference*. London: Abacus.

Gould, L. J., Stapley, L., & Stein, M. (2006). *The systems psychodynamics of organizations: Integrating the group relations approach, psychoanalytic, and open systems perspectives*. London: Karnac Books.

Kets De Vries, M.F.R., & Cheak, A. (2014). Psychodynamic Approach, *INSEAD Working Paper EMCCC*, 2.

Lehman, R., & van de Loo, E. (2015). Primary Task, Primary Risk and Social Defenses, core slide module 3 EMCCC, 8.

Long, S. (2013). *Socioanalytic Methods: Discovering the Hidden in Organisations and Social Systems*. London: Karnac.

Schein, Edgar H. (1980). *Foundations of modern psychology series Organizational psychology*. Englewood Cliffs, N.J. Prentice Hall.

Vansina, L., Vansina-Cobbaert, M.-J., Amado, G., & Schruijer, S. (2008). *Working across Organisational Boundaries: Understanding and Working with Inter-group Dynamics, in Psychodynamics for Consultants and Managers: From Understanding to Leading Meaningful Change*. Chichester, West Sussex, England: John Wiley & Sons, Ltd.

'The real voyage of discovery consists not in seeking new landscapes, but in having new eyes.'

– Marcel Proust

My concluding letter to you as a leader

Dear Leader,

I hope you have enjoyed this book. I hope this book has convinced you that the success rate of your strategy executing will increase by including a more radical human-centred perspective and tactics.

Before you put it down, and perhaps back on your shelf, I would like to wrap up with four questions that I hope will offer you reflection and motivation for action: Why this book? What is the essence of this book? Are you ready? What is next?

Why this book?

I assume most of you have experienced the challenge of realizing strategies successfully and have witnessed first-hand the ineffectiveness and inability to execute even the most well thought out strategies.

Strategy execution is complex. We know that roughly 70 percent of efforts at transformation fail. People in organizations struggle to focus on the right priorities, fail to act in accordance with the strategic objectives, or simply do not engage with the vision of the CEO. Often, people are not convinced about the importance and urgency of the change and simply do not buy-in to it. The financial losses resulting from failed strategy implementation are tremendous, not to mention the operational and emotional disruption caused to the organization and its people.

With so many consulting firms out there, so much literature published on the subject and the best practices available, why do most strategies still fail?

In my discussions with leaders of organizations, the challenges and frustrations channelled are mostly people related: Why is so much time, effort and energy of team members sidetracked by emotions, tensions, and conflicts? Why don't we get rid of the silos within my organization? Why do people in my organization not act and focus in accordance with our strategic objectives? Why do people in my organization not engage with the vision I shared? Why is my organization not ready to deal effectively with the rapidly changing challenges?

Values, beliefs and emotions have a proven impact on human motivation and thus influence our focus, decisions and actions. Yet these elements are often neglected in the professional world, thereby dehumanizing strategies and organizations.

: *What is the essence of this book?*

Emotion-based barriers present a major threat to strategy execution within many organizations. No strategy can afford to neglect emotional and psychological factors, because all strategies ultimately deal with people. I strongly believe and hopefully have convinced you that executing a strategy effectively requires going beyond fixing symptoms or introducing expensive short-term technical solutions. Interventions should start by exploring the root causes of the observed behaviours and integrating a solid business perspective complemented by psychology-informed approaches based on scientific tools. I believe in an approach that focuses on the visible technical elements such as structure, governance, processes and tools. Simultaneously, it is critical to tap into the world of values, beliefs, emotions, and hidden underlying motivational forces that influence individual and collective behaviour.

Why are emotions, values and beliefs often neglected in the strategic process? Why are they not part of the dominant logic of strategy execution of many leaders? I believe there are several reasons for this. Lack of knowledge and risk aversion of senior management play a role, but so does anxiety about dealing with emotions.

My mission is to have a different conversation with leaders and offer them a different approach to strategy execution. I work with leaders to solve their most critical issues by including human-centred strategies that work in their unique context. This experience was the basis for the book. I hope it provided you with new insights on how to humanize your organization and make your strategy really work. Based on leading research, real stories, real case studies and practical tools, I hope I made you more familiar with the world of human dynamics. I also hope you have a better understanding of how dealing consciously and effectively with these human dynamics might have a significant impact on the successful realization of your strategy.

IT IS POSSIBLE to have a team acting as ONE team (chapter 1). IT IS POSSIBLE to lead an organization where people work together spontaneously across teams (chapter 2). IT IS POSSIBLE to lead an organization where people act and focus in line with the strategy, set the right priorities and execute plans and decisions taken (chapter 3). IT IS POSSIBLE to be a leader who inspires and creates commitment to the strategy from within the organization (chapter 4). And yes, IT IS POSSIBLE to build a future-proof organization with efficiency, values, trust and fun at its heart (chapter 5).

Are you ready?

My three remaining questions for you: Are you serious about making your strategy a success? Do you have the patience to keep asking 'why'? Do you have the courage to take a less conventional approach?

What's next?

So, the big question, and one that you as a leader must answer every day: What do I do next?

We live in interesting times. In the Fourth Industrial Revolution, work and lives change more rapidly than ever before. I am convinced that organizations of tomorrow will live in a context of increased complexity, uncertainty, and continuous change. Organizations will be in a near-permanent state of organizational flux. In this era, I feel that the traditional way of executing strategy, as we have done in the past decennia, cannot keep up. Humanizing your strategy is not optional if you are to survive in this new reality.

Looking to this future, I would like to give you three final pieces of 'human' advice based on my experiences, what I have read, and the many interesting in-depth discussions with leaders like you. I'm convinced that applying these three pieces of advice will make your organization and you as a leader more successful.

1. Find the real issue, and root cause before you start solving it.

My advice to you is to 'keep asking why' for much longer. Nowadays, I find that all too often solutions are implemented that fix symptoms. They are expensive short-term technical solutions with limited to no impact. Now that you have read my book, you might want to focus more on the emotional and psychological factors at stake. Keep in mind that there is a rationale behind every human act – a logical explanation – even for actions that seem irrational. Also remember that there are different types of challenges requiring different approaches in solving them: adaptive challenges versus technical problems.

'Better to do a little well than a great deal badly.'
– Socrates

2. As a leader, be more self-aware about your own emotions and functioning.

Every day as a leader you make many decisions. These decisions involve interactions, and each of these can either support or harm the main effort of your organization. Be aware that because of the role modelling dimension you have as leader, the impact of a single behaviour on the whole organi-zation can be huge in a positive or negative sense. What I observe during interventions, and in coaching in particular, is that self-awareness of leaders is often low, especially on the emotional dimension. Moreover, remember that nothing is more central to who a person is than the way he or she reg-ulates and expresses emotions. It makes sense to create more awareness and understanding between what you do and why you do it and the impact of your behaviour on others and the organization overall. Self-reflection, introspection is a good starting point to create more awareness about your emotions and functioning as a leader.

> *'Mastering others is strength; mastering yourself is true power.'*
> – Lao Tzu

3. Never stop investing in trusted relationships and psychological safety.

Trust lies at the heart of effective interactions between people. As described in the chapters above, it is the foundation of effective collaboration and teamwork and leads to open and constructive dialogue, accountability, high performance and results. Psychological safety (can we take risks in this team without feeling insecure or embarrassed?) is far and away the most important dynamic for building high-performing teams and organizations. I experience that people often overestimate the level of trust between them. When you dig a little deeper (scratch the surface), you find that there is most often room for improvement. Investing in trust or psychological safety pays off.

> *'No passion so effectually robs the mind of all its powers*
> *of acting and reasoning as fear.'*
> – Edmund Burke

And finally, I hope you share my view on how much can be achieved by humanizing strategies, and on the risk of not doing this. I realize that the thinking about strategy realization needs to further evolve, and hope that, knowing what I know, you see that no strategy can afford to neglect emotional and psychological factors.

Good luck!

Geert Vercaeren

Email: humanizingstrategy@outlook.com
Website: www.humanizingstrategy.com

'Better to do a little well
than a great deal badly.'
— Socrates

About the author

Geert Vercaeren is a senior business consultant, coach and entrepreneur with 25 years of experience in leading complex business transformation, organizational development and HR transformation projects.

He has worked in close partnership with many corporations, public institutions, venture capital, family businesses and small and medium-sized enterprises. Examples of the larger organizations he has worked for are BASF, Total, ExxonMobil, Shell, Cargill, GSK, UCB, Johnson & Johnson, Shire-Takeda, Philips, Hewlett-Packard, Nissan, BNP Paribas Fortis, SWIFT, Umicore, bpost, ENGIE, Deloitte, The European Commission, etc.

Geert has taken up different leadership roles in leading consulting firms. During his 10 years at Deloitte, he was leading client projects, developing business and realizing significant growth of the Belgian consulting practice focusing on Strategic Change, Organization Transformation & Talent.

He graduated with distinction from INSEAD's Executive Masters degree in Organizational Psychology, holds an MA degree as Commercial Engineer, and a Co-active® Coaching certificate from The Coaches Training Institute.

Geert's mission is to work with leaders to solve their most critical issues by including human-centred strategies that work in their unique context. He wants to have a different conversation with leaders in organizations and offer them a different approach to strategy execution. In all of his work, he starts his project from the challenge and ambitions at business level and in addition integrates psychologically informed approaches focusing on underlying motivational forces, deeper sources of energy and behavioural patterns. He strongly believes it is key to understand deeper motivations and resistance to change and to uncover and tackle the root of potential dysfunction rather than to simply deal with its manifestations.

In his recent research at INSEAD, he explored the challenges of human dynamics of collaboration within and between organizations and how to maximize the success of initiatives to get rid of silo-working, silo mentality by integration a functional and psychological perspective in a hands-on approach.

Geert is the founder of B15, a consulting company dedicated to humanizing strategies (www.b15.be).

About the illustrator

Peter Moolan-Feroze trained as an artist at Camberwell School of Arts and Crafts, the Slade School (1979-1983), London University and then post-graduate at the Royal Academy Schools (1984-1987). He is fascinated with the idea of finding a synthesis between contrasting artistic elements such as form and colour, observation and invention, analysis and intuition.

While at the Royal Academy of Arts, Peter created the RA Outreach programme, taking creativity workshops with the artist's life model into schools nationwide. He ran this programme for twenty years, staged three exhibitions of young people's work at the Academy and as a result was asked to contribute to executive programmes at the London Business School.

For the last fifteen years, he has been an external consultant at the London Business School where he helps leaders and managers to understand more about the nature of creativity and the connection between art and business. He has designed creative learning programmes for companies including Deutsche Bank, A.T. Kearney, Givaudan, M&S, McLaren Automotive, Unilever, Estée Lauder and Jo Malone. Peter believes in Renaissance thinking and in the power of cross fertilization between subjects, encouraging managers to realize that solutions can occur by employing subjects outside your own skill base.

For this book, Peter constructed narratives around some of the key messages in the five chapters. They informed the ideas behind the drawings, which all explore different human aspects of performance in business.

A word of thanks

Writing a first book is quite something. To be honest, at the start of the process, I did not know if I would like the process of writing a book, if I would be able to do it and if I'd stay motivated. Looking back, I can say it was a fascinating journey.

Firstly, it helped me a great deal to take distance and reflect on how I can bring most value in partnering with leaders of organizations to solve their most critical issues and in reaching their ambitions. Writing the stories confronted me with the fact that something essential is missing in today's mainly rational professional logic; no business strategy can afford to neglect emotional and psychological factors. I also realized that many business leaders today still lack knowledge of how to deal with the human side of change or are anxious about dealing with emotions. This gave me the motivation to write this book and kept me going. I wanted to put my stories, experiences and perspectives on paper in a pragmatic way and share these with you.

First of all, I am very grateful to my business relations and clients for the trust they gave me in working together day in and out to solve their most challenging issues. Our projects together are an important source of inspiration for this book.

I also like to thank my colleagues. The deep business and psychological expertise we bring together during our projects combined with our common mindset and high professional standards is a key differentiator in the value we bring to our clients. You make the work we do impactful and fun.

My thanks goes to Manfred Kets de Vries, Roger Lehman and Erik Van De Loo from INSEAD for their inspiration and for immersing me in the interesting world of systems psychodynamics. My fascination with behavioural dynamics as drivers for organizational performance derives largely from them. I would also like to thank my INSEAD EMCC (Executive Master in Coaching and Consulting for Change) classmates for providing a sounding board and for their friendship.

As special thanks goes to Bert Smits for sharing his experiences of writing books and for putting me in touch with Lannoo. This is how it all started.

I would like to thank my publisher LannooCampus, Niels Janssens and Lotte Demeyer in particular, for their unfailing belief in me and their valuable support throughout the entire process of writing this book. Also, thanks to Glenn Geeraerts for providing his senior advice on the structure and content of the book, and Anna Rich for editing and commenting on every chapter, section, page and sentence.

Thank you, Peter, for the beautiful art illustrations you made for each chapter. They bring an extra dimension and value to this book.

Thanks to my parents for their endless love, care, support and belief in me.

Last, but certainly not least, my heartfelt thanks goes to my wife Leen, daughters Hannah, Marie and Saar, and close family for their support in creating the time and space to make this happen.

D/2021/45/73 – ISBN 978 94 014 7499 3 – NUR 801

COVER AND INTERIOR DESIGN LetterLust | Stefaan Verboven

LannooCampus Publishers is a subsidiary of Lannoo Publishers,
the book and multimedia division of Lannoo Publishers nv.

LannooCampus Publishers
Vaartkom 41 box 01.02   P.O. Box 23202
3000 Leuven   1100 DS Amsterdam
Belgium   Netherlands